The Secret Life of Love and Sex

Making relationships work and
what to do if they don't

The Secret Life of Love and Sex

Making relationships work and
what to do if they don't

Terence Watts

**PSYCHE
BOOKS**

Winchester, UK
Washington, USA

First published by Psyche Books, 2014
Psyche Books is an imprint of John Hunt Publishing Ltd., Laurel House, Station Approach,
Alresford, Hants, SO24 9JH, UK
office1@jhpbooks.net
www.johnhuntpublishing.com
www.psyche-books.com

For distributor details and how to order please visit the 'Ordering' section on our website.

Design: Stuart Davies

Printed and bound by CPI Group (UK) Ltd, Croydon, CR0 4YY

We operate a distinctive and ethical publishing philosophy in all areas of our business, from our global network of authors to production and worldwide distribution.

CONTENTS

This book is dedicated to

Measle, Bertie and Pansy

Who all contribute so greatly to the richness of my life

Foreword

This book is engrossing to the point that time passes far more quickly than you realise while you're reading it. From the opening chapter which poses an important question – which most will never have considered – right at the beginning, to the closing paragraphs which inspire much thought, this is a fascinating and enjoyable read.

It becomes clear almost straight away that to enjoy a satisfying and successful relationship you have to first truly know yourself, and I defy anybody not to be surprised at what they discover about themselves in these pages! As soon as you start reading about the three major personality types, the Warrior, the Settler and the Nomad, you start to recognise your true self, the part you might have kept hidden for years... and with that comes a staggering insight into why things don't always work out the way you want them to.

It is a fact that discovering why we behave in the way we do towards others, and why we react to them as we do, can provide an astonishingly clear insight into almost every aspect of relationships. So much so, that this book should be required reading for all those who are about to embark on a romance, whether it's for the first, twenty-first or fifty-first time. You will discover more easily than you thought possible how to recognise the truth about the one you are preparing to entrust your emotions to before it's too late!

But it's not just about getting into a relationship in the first place. It's about how to sustain the feeling of love and affection that we usually start out with, or how to rekindle them if they've faded. More importantly, perhaps, it's also about how to easily extricate yourself from a pairing that has passed its 'sell by' date or has become abusive.

The whole gamut of the relationship game is covered here;

how to make sure you choose the right partner in the first place, how to keep sex alive and joyful, how to confidently sort out sexual difficulties, how to argue without ending up in the divorce courts – and the times when a lie or a secret is a good thing and the other times when it will come back to haunt you. It even covers a whole host of common problems that are often 'prickly' to deal with and shows the reader how to address them in such a way that there is a positive outcome instead of an argument.

Of course, not all relationships have a happy ending and when things go awry we can so easily descend into a welter of self-pity and self-recrimination that stops us from moving on for far too long. But there is even help for that unhappy circumstance here, help that can soon have you picking yourself up, brushing yourself down, and raring to move on to something new and spectacular – because this book can help you find just that!

Dame Emma Jane Brown

Dame Emma Jane Brown is a former international show-jumper who was ranked the best female rider in Great Britain for many years. Winner of numerous championships, she represented her country in the Nations Cup no less than 13 times. After illness ended her career prematurely she has worked as a commentator for Sky and Eurosport, a columnist for several women's and lifestyle magazines and as a tireless charity ambassador. Emma received a knighthood for services to equestrianism in Malta in 2011 and runs a luxury concierge and events company.

Chapter One

The biggest surprise of all...

Is your partner a rival or a friend?

The question might never have occurred to you until this minute but even as you think about this, you can probably work it out. Now, because you are reading this book, it is likely that you are unhappy with your situation but the important thing to take on board at this very moment is that you actually chose it. Argue if you must, but as this chapter unfolds you will begin to recognise that this is a great truth and understanding it can change your life.

Even if you are currently solo, reflecting on past relationships will provide a clue – they are all likely to have had similarities when you examine them closely enough. It makes no difference whether it was what you actually wanted or not; something about that individual was attractive to you and it is all part of the package, rivalry, friendship and every uncomfortable thing else included. Take responsibility for your choice and you are already on your way to making a better one. Of course, in all relationships, there is a delicately-tuned balance of emotions and attitudes. When that balance truly works for both partners then there is harmony, even if that harmony is a bit 'spiky' at times; when it does not, then mayhem is on the cards! That is usually when things start to fall apart and so often continue to do so until the inevitable parting of the ways.

The difficulties arise out of a very simple situation, in that the first and probably the only training we are given on how to handle this most complex of human endeavours is usually at the hands of those least well-equipped to teach us – our parents. They, of course, were taught by their parents, who were taught by *their* parents, who were taught by... well, you get the picture.

The lessons get some modification on each 'round' as a result of 'modernisation' or mutually exclusive conflicts, so what we actually learn is a mish-mash of ideas that have become somehow accepted as the norm.

Sometimes, it gets particularly complicated: one parent teaches us one thing – that it is actually okay to be deceitful if the partner does not know about it, for instance – while the other teaches us exactly the opposite. Then we have to decide for ourselves what to do and usually end up with a confused feeling about whether what we are doing is okay or not okay. The result of that might well be a 'guilt trip', some defensive aggression, or a very robust re-apportionment of responsibility for the situation: *"Well, it wouldn't have happened if you hadn't..."* or sometimes: *"Hah! Well what about what **you** do then?"* That sort of blame-shifting response is usually bad news as far as the long-term survival of the relationship is concerned.

Although we do not really notice it, we are taught things like:

- Whether a partner is a competitor or an ally.
- What we are 'supposed' to do if our partner displeases us.
- What to do if our partner has a different viewpoint from our own.
- Which feelings should be expressed and which should be suppressed.
- If it is okay to lie and cheat sometimes or if we must always be honest.
- If we should argue to win, or to try to solve a problem.
- If sexuality is a good thing, a bad thing, or unimportant (usually, this is learnt from parents' attitudes to television programmes, 'disguised' conversations, how we are told **what** we are told about the subject, and other covert teachings.)

We start the process from the moment we come into the world, learning in the most profound way possible – experience and example, and at the end of it all, we have a clear idea of how things usually work or are 'supposed' to work. The problem is that what we have absorbed is all based on our own life, hopes, fears and aspirations and never mind what anybody else wants. Actually, of course, what anybody else wants is based on their life, hopes, fears and aspirations, which will be quite different from our own.

The surprise is not so much that things frequently do not work out – it is that they so often do!

For most of us, the training leaves out a Great Truth: **Relationships are a joint effort.**

When something is not working properly, it is not working for *both* halves of the couple, even if one half does not realise it; when a couple argue, they are in disagreement with *each other* – yet both are likely to feel that their partner is disagreeing with *them*. Criticism, mind games, bullying and ridicule from either partner are potent indicators of a dangerous instability, for unless both halves of a couple are trying to move in the same direction *together* most of the time at least, the relationship will eventually collapse. Even the collapse does not always work well, though, and then the liaison struggles on well past its 'sell by' date.

Sex – a vital part

One of the most difficult of areas to cope with is sex; it is fair to say that most established relationships are less than totally satisfactory for one or both partners, even if everything was amazing in the beginning.

This is not a book about sex but it does access the subject in some detail later on; for now, just accept that it is a *vital part* of a relationship, even where there has been a decision to remain celibate. The drive for sexual activity is impossible to ignore and indeed, it should not be ignored. It is a fundamental life instinct, the importance of which should be properly understood and respected for what it is... for without it, you would not even exist. The sexual instinct carries the second strongest urge known to mankind – the first is survival of self – and it is not just the males, either, but *both* genders, even though their responses and attitudes are quite different. When relationships cannot start or when they repeatedly founder, it is almost certain that sex, or a misunderstanding of some aspect of it, comes into the frame in some way or another.

The problem is, that although most relationships are lacking in some way in the sexual department, it is all too easy to believe that it is only *our* relationship that has the problem and that it is actually more to do with our partner than ourselves. When things are not going well, it is all too easy to believe the 'advertising' that some would-be new sexual partner gives us about their prowess, appetite, and level of understanding. All too easy to believe that they are always ready, often manage to have multiple orgasms, or sometimes 'just enjoy a cuddle without it having to turn into sex.' Like all advertisers, they tell us what we want to hear and we can easily fall for it... but if we get sucked into it, the reality is so often a let-down when we find ourselves in the same old, same old situation yet again.

And that is exactly what this book is about. Learning how to avoid that same old, same old situation and instead get into and sustain a relationship that works, not just in sexuality but across the board. Learning how to *be* in a relationship that works. It will even help you discover how to – elegantly – leave a relationship that is not working. If you tend to always find the 'wrong' sort of partner, then this book is for you; if you have never been able to establish a good relationship, then this book is for you; in fact, if your experience with relationships is uncomfortable in any way at all, this book is for you!

You will be able to gain recognition of the destructive lessons you learnt when you were growing up and by understanding them, be empowered to make vital changes. You will grow in confidence and self-esteem as you begin to realise that the things you might have blamed yourself for in the past were simply the result of those early lessons – but let us not blame your parents for your problems, because *their* relationship might well have worked for them! They came from a different time, when life was different, and the past, as someone once said, is a different country...

Although it might seem unlikely at this stage, it is entirely possible to make amazing changes to the way your relationships function. So:

- If you are already in a rocky relationship, you might be able to fix it.
- If your relationships have never worked out, there is a good chance that the next one will.
- If you always seem to end up with the 'wrong' sort of person, next time will be different.
- If you tend to stay in a relationship when you really want out, you will not have to do that any more.
- If sex causes a problem, you will discover how to sort it out.
- Any form of relationship anxiety will become a thing of the past.
- Needy and insecure behaviour can be banished.

Belief and expectation...

Although most people do not realise it, the process of belief and expectation that operates deep in the subconscious mind has a profound effect on relationships. The importance of this process is well known in the world of psychology because it affects the outcome of almost everything we do or try to do. We are not talking about everyday physical situations here, things like expecting the car to start when we turn the key, but about the workings of what we can think of as our 'inner self', the real self with all its fears, anxieties and hang-ups.

It is a fact that subconscious processes are far more powerful than conscious thought. If, at a deep level, we believe we can achieve a goal and expect to achieve it, then the odds are that we *will* achieve it, as long as what we are seeking is feasible. There is a catch, however... the subconscious mind is completely non-selective and will operate on a bad idea just as certainly as it will on a good idea. It is completely impartial and takes little account of what we consciously want to happen. Not only that, it is invisible to our conscious and we are not able to truly know what truths and beliefs are buried in there! If there is a belief that we are in some way an unlucky person, then we expect to be unlucky, and we actually look for unlucky – and we will find unlucky. After all, we were not looking for anything else so would not have noticed it if we bumped into it – we keep on looking until we find what we subconsciously believe and expect we will find, even if we consciously want something quite different. We might well consciously wish to be lucky... but if that 'inner self' has learnt that luck is undesirable or undeserved, then we will find anything but. Sometimes, we might be vaguely aware that we are not really expecting to find what we are looking for; we have a feeling that it will not work *for us*. We might look at somebody we *really* like but in the same moment know they would not be interested in us. That is belief and expectation at work.

Those subconscious processes are based on every life experience we have encountered; we start to absorb ideas into our subconscious from the moment we are born and they gradually build up the internal database of what we can do and cannot do, can have and cannot have, how we fit into the world, how others view us, and so on. These things become part of our personal belief and expectation system. Be sure not to underestimate the importance of all this because:

- If you believe you are loveable you will expect to be loved and you will unconsciously search out somebody who will love you.
- If you believe you are not worthy of love, you will expect not to be loved, and although consciously you might **think** that you are searching for 'the one', you will unconsciously seek out somebody who will not love you – usually somebody else who believes they are unloveable.

That second circumstance is interesting; so often, when somebody thinks themselves to be unloveable, they appear to punish their partner for it. It is as if they are seeking to prove to themselves that they are not worthy of love and in so doing behave in a manner that is calculated to arouse emotional responses that are far from the love they consciously seek.

It is highly probable that if you have difficulties with relationships, then you fall into that 'I am unloveable' category. This is almost always the case, though it might not be what you perceive with your conscious thoughts. Consciously, you might believe that you are: *a 'bad' person; weird; substandard; awkward; not sexy; too inhibited; too aggressive or bolshie; jinxed; a disaster; selfish; a doormat; stupid; ridiculous; odd...* or some other negatively descriptive concept.

Translated, any of those concepts will confirm the core belief of: *"I am unloveable."* If you are doubtful about this, just try thinking to yourself, or saying out loud: *"I am unloveable because I'm..."* and add those concepts from the list one at a time. If one of them feels uncomfortable, it is because it is touching a belief in the subconscious. If it produces tears, then it is a deeply-held belief. Either way, you must begin now to understand something of vital importance:

*You actually **learnt** to think like that during your formative years. It might not have been the case that you were **supposed** to take that lesson on board in that way at such a deep level. It was just your* *perception at the time for whatever reason. You believed it and therefore begun to expect it and are now doing your best to find it. Your subconscious knows the **exact** signs and indicators that you have found somebody who will confirm your belief and will ensure that you feel an attraction towards them – and that attraction can be immensely powerful.*

The sad thing is that that subconscious negative belief is always wrong because, in truth, very few people would *genuinely* possess even one of those negative attributes in that list, and if they did they would be likely to be totally unaware of that fact. Now, here is a great truth: You must believe you are loveable before you can expect to be loved.

That last sentence is very important. Just occasionally, more by luck than judgment or selection, somebody who believes they are unloveable stumbles unwittingly into a relationship where they *are* loved. There are many reasons how and why this might happen but they are not important right at this moment. What *is* important is that the individual simply cannot recognise or believe that they are loved and cannot therefore act accordingly. The relationship does not 'fit' that which they know is the 'norm' for them and instead of finding joy in what they have, they might be suspicious, cynical, doubtful, testing, unfaithful or just downright bad mannered.

Whatever they do and however they do it, they will usually wreck the relationship without ever having realised that they actually had what they were consciously searching for. At the end of it all, they will say something like: *"Well, I knew it was too good to be true right at the beginning,"* or: *"Why on earth do I always mess up – I must be just a waste of space."* And so the belief is reinforced, ready for the next encounter.

But this book is not just about getting you to realise you are capable of being, and probably already are, a loveable person; it is about helping you to understand the mistakes to which you are prone so that you can stop making them. It is about helping you to understand the true dynamics of a relationship. To that end, it is useful to understand why on earth you would have been taught such damaging ideas about self and relationships in the first place and also why you have taken them on board at such a deep level.

The strongest instinct of all

We will look first at the reason you so readily accepted those negative ideas and made them your own. It can actually be summed up in a single word. **SURVIVAL**

To survive, we must emulate our elders – after all, they are the only teachers we have in the beginning and they know everything, or so it seems to us. We try to do what they do and when we cannot do that, we try to do what we believe they want us to do. We must keep them happy at all costs, for without them we will perish. They know the world and they know how to survive so we had jolly well better follow their plan in order to do so ourselves. If they teach us something about ourselves, we must take it into account, good or bad, and act accordingly.

If a lesson is repeated over and again, we cease to question it; it is as if the subconscious understands that it must be an important facet for survival. The lesson learned becomes part of what might be called our *functional mode*, our natural way of being; it becomes part of that database of self, the storehouse of everything we can and cannot do, should and should not have or expect to have.

Now, the subconscious has one more trick up its sleeve; it stores all this information behind an almost impenetrable barrier called the **Conscious Critical Faculty – CCF** for short. If a bit of information comes in from the outside world that contradicts that which is already established there by repetition (or sometimes trauma) it is instantly rejected. This is why the person who believes they are, for instance, stupid, will vigorously defend themselves against any attempt to show them otherwise.

It is just the same if the belief is that they are unlovable, weird, ugly, not sexy... and the rest. And even that rather odd process is all about survival, for if what you have always done has always worked (and it clearly has because you are still here) then you had better continue to do it. Any change would lead to unknown territory and heaven knows what might happen then! So we seek to avoid it at all costs. Stay with what we know and understand, and we have security... but in that fact is one of the biggest problems of life and relationships: **Security is not based on that which is good but on that which is familiar.**

This is the reason why so many people stay in a poor relationship; it is simply what they are used to and what they subconsciously believe is acceptable. They are trapped by *destructive security.* Quite often, they will justify their position with a well-known bit of rationalisation: *"Better the Devil you know..."* And who knows? For them, that might well be the case. Until they somehow get behind that *almost* impenetrable **CCF** and learn otherwise. Until they start to question whether or not what they have always believed about self is actually so or if it is just an idea they were given for some reason or another. Will you do that?

Why teach *that?*

And so we come to the second important facet of the lessons you received about self and relationships – why on earth would anybody teach you such negative values? Well, most of the time, lessons of that sort are given without any real intent or knowledge of the outcome and are purely egocentric, based on nothing more than the way the teacher (usually parent) is feeling at the time. A bitter or sad person, for instance, may well discharge their bitterness or sadness at the person who is least likely to fight back and make those feelings worse – their child. This is not based on a desire to wound or destroy but is purely a discharge of the way the parent is feeling at that moment in time.

In your own life, it only ever told you about your parent and nothing about *you*. It told you of the sense of inadequacy and frustration that the parent was feeling and that is based on *their* life, hopes, fears and desires going back to before you were even born.

You never were responsible for the way your parents felt in life. Even when phrases, statements and concepts were repeated incessantly, as is often the case, it still was only about your parent's emotional state, about what he or she was feeling, and absolutely nothing to do with *you*. You never were responsible for the way your parents felt in life; that was established long before you were even thought of and their behaviour was nothing more than a reflection of their own early teaching.

But, you had no way of knowing that and so you believed what you were told and continued to believe it as it found its way behind that CCF.

Sometimes, the lessons are subtly different, taught by example and observation. What we see our parents doing we have to assume is the proper thing to do, the way we have to try to be if we are to survive. It matters not whether what we observe is violence, love, resentment, sharing, humiliation, closeness, contempt... we store it all as the way to be in that personal database. Sometimes we react *against* what we have been taught, so that an abused person becomes a carer, for example (though that circumstance is probably born out of an urge to care for self) but it makes no difference – we are still reacting to the lessons we have been taught.

Complicated... not!

It might seem to you now that trying to change is far too complicated to even think about. In fact, though, it is a far easier task than continuing to survive and try to find happiness with the uncomfortable set of ideas and concepts that you have been working with up until now! All it needs is:

- A willingness to accept that if things keep on going wrong then you are a part of that 'going wrongness'.
- A willingness to examine the ideas you have been given about self and relationships and then to make changes where necessary – and that is going to be far easier than you could ever have imagined.

The work starts in the very next chapter...

Chapter Two

What are you like...?

Supposing there is a secret you?

It might be that you often think there is a different you 'in there' somewhere that just doesn't get out much, if at all. This could be the you that can get great things out of life, including a fantastic relationship, but it is the you that somehow never quite manages to show itself to anybody. Or maybe it is only a part of you that is secret. The 'visible' part that the world knows about chooses things and situations that you know others would approve of, while the *real* you wants something – or somebody – completely different and hang what others might make of it!

Even if you disagree with all this, it is likely that you do not truly know yourself; most people do not. What you *think* you are like is all down to that teaching that you read about in the last chapter... but almost certainly that is not the real you at all, even though you will behave as if it is.

Understanding certain things can make huge differences to your entire life and perception of self. For instance, if you were taught that you were stubborn, you might prefer to believe that you are actually tenacious; if you were led to believe that you are not single-minded enough, you might feel better when you recognise your adaptability; if you were told that you were too noisy, perhaps you can revel in your enthusiasm. There is always a positive side to every negative.

So in this chapter we are going to set about discovering the real you. That can be both exhilarating and daunting, and for good reason, for it is a fact that the way you do anything is the way you do everything. Now, if you are not too sure about that rather bold statement, think about the way you do two different tasks and then compare them. It shows up even in simple things like eating and talking; if you speak rather quickly, for example, then you probably eat quickly, too. And it is odds on that if you drive a car you do that fast, as well. Even more, you probably hate waiting for anything... but perhaps you speak slowly and steadily, in which case the same probably applies to eating and driving – and waiting for something is not a problem.

All of this is very important for two reasons:

- If you are doing things in a way that is not really suited to you it means that your relationships will be affected in the same way.
- When you permanently change one thing, especially the way you see yourself, all sorts of other things will gradually change as well.

At just about this point, some people might start to argue, claiming that none of this could possibly apply to them and anyway, they are not interested in changing their life – they just want to make relationships work better than they have done in the past.

Well, if you are thinking like that, that's what's known as *resistance to change* and it is entirely normal. Change might well worry you a little... or a lot. Until you stop to realise that if you keep on doing what you have always done, you will always get what you always got. So let us plump for exciting instead of daunting! Let us start to discover that the change you are going to find is not scary at all but absolutely enlightening and liberating.

Three primary colours

Just as there are only three primary colours that make up all of the millions of different hues that you can see in life, so there are three primary types of personality, the mix of which governs how every single person functions. The short personality test given here will provide the starting point on your own journey of self-discovery and so that you can refer to it later, you should write the answers down rather than decide you will remember them.

It is a good idea to do the test before reading any further if you want to avoid the risk of an artificial result; for that reason, too, think hard about your answers and promise yourself you will not change them later on! It's important to understand that there is no best, highest, most likely, least likely, better, or anything else, so do remember to choose each answer that is closest to how you actually are and not as you think you 'should' be:

Question 1: If you had to choose only one of these, would you choose to be (a) **rich,** (b) **loved,** or (c) **famous?**

Question 2: If you were suddenly rich and you had to choose only one of these, would you prefer to: (a) **save it,** (b) **share it,** or (c) **spend it?**

Question 3: Say where that part of you that you call 'me' or 'I' actually 'lives' in your body: (a) **head,** (b) **heart,** or (c) **somewhere else.**

Answer question 4 only if you have one of each 'a', 'b', or 'c' answer – it is only here to ensure an accurate definition.

Question 4: Which of these would you least hate people to think about you: (a) **assertive and awkward,** (b) **meek and mild,** or (c) **showy and loud?**

You probably have an assortment of a, b and/or c answers but if they are all the same, or if you have one letter missing, that is absolutely fine, as you will discover later on. The important thing is that you must have been honest with what you selected, so if you are not quite sure about that, do go back and check again before continuing.

We will come back to your answers later on but right now, we will look at those three 'colours' of personality. We will also give them names and later on you will discover where they came from.

- The first we can call **'Warrior',** all to do with strength, control, and getting things done.
- The second is **'Settler',** concerned with sorting things out and negotiating with others to make the best of situations.
- Third, we have '**Nomad'**, associated with energy, inventiveness and inspirational enthusiasm for life.

Of course, each one has negative attributes, too, and you will discover what those are as you look at the profile of each type. Before we go any further, though, it is time that you discovered which of the three you truly are, at heart.

If you have more 'a' answers, even if it is only one more than the others, then you are predominantly **Warrior;** more 'b' answers reveal you to be a **Settler,** while more 'c' answers show that you are a **Nomad.** The more of any letter that you have, the stronger that influence will be, though you will still show some of the traits associated with any other letters in your profile.

Now we will look at what it all means. In the following descriptions, the more answers you have for each one, the more of those characteristics you will show *or will have available to you even if you didn't realise it until now.* Even if all your answers show the same letter, though, there will still be a few attributes from the other two that you can identify with, though they can always be over-ridden by the dominant trait when necessary.

The descriptions given here give you the overall 'feel' of the personality and 'way of being' associated with each type. Gradually, as you read through the rest of the book, you will discover more detailed information about each one and discover how a relationship with them would work when taking your own profile into account.

Remember that there is no 'best' or 'better' so resist any urge to go back and change your answers, whatever the reason – all that means, if you feel it, is that you have been trying to behave in a way that simply isn't the real you. It never works successfully, especially in relationships, and if you continue to shy away from that 'secret you' then you continue to shy away from the perfect partner. Remember what you read in the last chapter: **Relationships are a joint effort.** This means that for it to be happy, you have to be with somebody who wants someone just like you. And think about what that means for a moment:

- You never have to pretend you like something you do not.
- You never have to pretend you are at ease when you are not.
- You do not have to think how to be.
- You know that you are giving the best you have to your partner.
- You can always say what you want to say without fear.
- You do not have to keep part of you secret.
- You can relax and be the real you all the time.

Now it's time to look at those profiles:

The Warrior

Positive traits: Resourceful; perceptive; self-sufficient; generally sensible; determined; tenacious; direct; careful.

Negative traits: Critical; uncommunicative; manipulative; cynical; controlling; difficulty in admitting error.

Personality style: The Warrior is usually a logical and analytically orientated type of person. They are a steadfast friend to those they trust, though that trust has to be earned – they do not bond with others easily. There is a tendency to question most things, even the questions that others might ask them, and they will quickly see the flaws in any plan, situation or argument.

They frequently have a reputation for firmness with a 'bark that is worse than their bite'. Less emotionally orientated than the other two groups – they are a not a particularly 'warm' sort of personality – they therefore tend to be less concerned about what others think of them, which is why they have no difficulty in taking charge of all sorts of situations. Expressing emotion other than the various forms of irritation is difficult for this group though this is not to say that they do not feel it. They *do* fall deeply in love but may not be fully aware of it and are certainly not quick to say so. They dislike silliness or thoughtlessness and do not suffer fools gladly, if at all.

Though difficult to get along with on occasions they are not actually unpleasant people and can be quite charming while things are going their way. It is when life or their environment is not behaving itself in the required manner that their underlying personality will be inclined to assert itself somewhat abruptly. In a determinedly negative mood, especially when it has been 'triggered' by somebody else, they can often be somewhat intimidating, abrupt, intolerant or even downright rude!

The Settler

Positive traits: Caring; usually cheerful; pleasant; communicative; tolerant; adaptable; helpful; makes the best of things; finds the best in people.

Negative traits: Under-confident; tendency to depression and/or mood swings; gives up easily; refuses to say what is wrong.

Personality style: The Settler is a complicated but responsive 'people person', governed by feelings, in touch with their emotions and easy to get along with. There is often a distinct tendency towards being a 'social chameleon' fitting in with and sharing in whatever is going on around them at any one time. They are adaptable, always being able to 'make the best of a bad job', and have a horror of being disliked or of upsetting others. Highly intuitive, they often know what somebody *really* means, even if they are not saying it, and on occasions can appear to have ESP or a 'sixth-sense'.

The most obvious thing about the Settler personality is a pleasant and responsive attitude. They are tactful and careful with the feelings of other people, though there is often a marked tendency to 'cut off their nose to spite their face', an 'all or nothing' approach, in which if they cannot have *absolutely* what they want, they will simply refuse to have any part of it at all. When confident, they are excellent communicators, and totally without equal when it comes to having an instinctive grasp of all that is going on around them. They are usually unexciting though reliable, and more often than not come over as the nice – in the best sense of the word – people that they are. Negatively, they can suffer from what might be described as the 'doormat syndrome' in which they are continually taken advantage of in some way, and though they grumble about it, they make no effort to redress the situation.

They are not always as soft as they seem, though; they cannot abide injustice or unfairness and will fight somebody else's battle far more readily than their own. If they win their battle, they will often try to make a friend out of their erstwhile enemy with a 'let bygones be bygones' attitude.

The Nomad

Positive: Enthusiastic; uplifting for others; often inventive; outgoing; inspiring; optimistic; persuasive.

Negative: Boastful; exaggerates most things; unreliable and/or irresponsible; cannot abide waiting for anything.

Personality style: The Nomad personality needs to be different from the crowd in some way, preferably in many ways. Usually charismatic, they tend to be lively, noisy, and high-spirited; they may sometimes be determinedly 'slob-like', though, since this is still an expression of individuality. They can be Actors (with a capital 'A') all the time, and adore all the attention they can get. The boredom threshold is low and there must always be something exciting happening to or for this personality – and it doesn't matter much whether it is good or bad, for they can glory in disaster. There is usually little in the way of 'hidden depths' so that what you see is what you get, with few complications other than occasional irresponsibility.

They are often multi-faceted, associated with all sorts of diverse situations and seem determined to enjoy to the full – and they generally succeed. Quite often, they provide uplift and inspiration for a great many others along the way, thanks to their expressive nature, which often leads to them being good lecturers or teachers, in which professions they seem to be able to overcome their tendency towards irresponsibility.

Perhaps surprisingly, they can also do well in law and finance, probably because these areas are as far removed from the emotional side of life as they can be. The Nomad does not 'do' emotions much better than the Warrior, though they may very well act a thoroughly convincing part under certain circumstances, especially if it is in their own interests to do so. They are much more forthcoming than the Warrior, though, in expressing their feelings, especially if it is about themselves. Fun, pleasure and self-gratification are important, though they can seem truly astonished and hurt if these traits are criticised; to them, they are just being totally 'normal'. Negatively, they can be melodramatic, excessively exuberant or excitable, and prone to child-like temper outbursts, the like of which has to be seen to be believed!

Whilst not the most reliable of individuals as a rule, they are quite often not as irresponsible as they at first seem. There is a tendency to act first and think afterwards, with little difficulty in changing a course of action.

Who are you really?

Now you've read the profiles, you will have realised that you show something of each of the types. This is not really surprising, of course, since we are all human and they are all 'normal' human traits. At this point there are three possible situations in response to what you have read so far:

- The profile you have read does not really seem like you at all.
- It is like you but you keep some of it hidden a lot of the time.
- It is like you and you already 'let it all hang out'.

We will examine each of these situations to see what it means as far as relationships are concerned.

Not really like you

Although you might feel that you are not really like the profile that you are 'supposed' to be according to the personality test, that is probably not the case. After all, you answered the questions! Remember that statement 'the way you do anything is the way you do everything'? Well, that is why those questions are likely to produce an accurate assessment. They are the same sort of questions that many professional psychologists and other 'people workers' use to assess their client's potential; some of them even use that exact process. Of course, no test is perfect so if you are absolutely certain that one of the other profiles describes you exactly, then 'adopt' that one instead. As long as you are certain...

For the moment, though, we will assume that it is accurate, in which case there are three uncomfortable possibilities:

- If you are really a Warrior but have to act as either of the other two, your deeper self will be irritated by those that you attract, which will lead to arguments and friction. You might be attracted to Warrior types and that is a disaster, as you will see later.
- If you are really a Nomad but have to act otherwise, your relationships will falter very quickly because you attract people who do not stimulate you at all, instead of those who 'feed' your deeper needs. You might be attracted to

Nomads, which is almost as bad as the Warrior with Warrior combination.

• If you are really a Settler masquerading as Warrior or Nomad, then you will fall into relationships that make you anxious in some way. You might be drawn to Settlers, only to discover that the relationship soon becomes boring or jaded.

In the next chapter, you will discover how to make sure you find the best partner for you and how to make the relationship work well, right from the beginning. Now, though, we will look at why you might have suppressed your true personality.

There are really only two possible reasons. One is that over a period of time in your younger years, you discovered that being you was in some way undesirable and resulted in some sort of punishment or disapproval; the second is that you had to adopt a particular stance in order to 'stand your ground' with other members of the family.

Maybe your parents (or whoever brought you up) and any siblings were delightful, kind and truly nice people... who showed sad disappointment which made you feel guilty if you did something in a different way to what they wanted. Or perhaps they were dictatorial so that their way was the only way and they showed abundant anger if you did not behave yourself as they demanded. Either situation can be very persuasive as far as changing your behaviour goes. Of course, it could have been something between the two and it is not important whether or not you can remember the situation; that was then and this is now!

Then, there was no choice. You were brought into the parent/child relationship with no say in the matter and if you had to modify your behaviour to get the best out of it, then that was a good thing to do.

Now, there *is* choice. It is not a good thing at all, if you want a loving relationship, to try to behave in a way that is not really you. Far better to trust that the real you is truly worthy of your partner's love and affection.

Later, we will consider how you can go about gradually making the changes you need and preparing for a better future.

You keep some of it hidden

The only parts of you that are best kept 'under wraps' are attitudes and behaviours that you know beyond doubt are socially undesirable. Almost always, though, what somebody chooses to keep hidden is in fact an absolutely normal aspect of personality. That they consider it to be unacceptable is likely to be based solely on the fact that somebody else did not like it and vigorously stressed the 'badness' of it. You might have been quick to point out the flaws and contradictions in arguments, for example, and been admonished firmly that you were a rude and bad-mannered individual, when the reality is that you are perceptive and a straight-talker. There are many people who appreciate those particular qualities.

Maybe you were criticised for being 'too excitable' and not sticking to anything for long enough, when the truth is that you are enthusiastic with a wide range of interests – and a lot of people find that sort of lively nature endearing and lovable. Or perhaps you were constantly reminded that you were a bit 'soft' and far too easy going; and yet softness and tolerance are wonderful attributes to bring to a relationship with the right person.

Remember that when you were young, it might well have been a good idea to fit into what others wanted but now you are an adult, you can learn to positively revel in being your true self and being loved for who you really are.

You let it all hang out

It is a good thing that you make no attempt to disguise yourself in any way but the fact that you are reading this book does indicate that it is not really working as far as relationships are concerned. There are two possible reasons for this. One is that you are determined to have everything your own way and do not intend to be even a little flexible; the second is that you somehow manage to choose the 'wrong' sort of partner. Usually, when this is the case, it is because you are gravitating towards people whom you believe others will approve of, partners that others might actually choose for you.

This is not at all an uncommon situation, especially where there has been tight parental control during your formative years. It might even be that you are drawn to individuals whom you know your friends would like or admire, though that might be a totally subconscious process. There is a very powerful indicator of that situation and it is this: *you are usually not interested in anybody who shows an evident interest in you.*

Because you already know yourself quite well, you do not have to make very much change to the way you are, though you do need to re-evaluate what you are searching for. If it is usually you who ends your relationships, then it is likely that you are not choosing well in the first place; if it is usually your partner who finishes it all, then it is probable that the way you *appear* to be from the outside does not 'fit' with the way you actually are. In other words, what they see is *not* what they get.

Becoming the real you

So now you are beginning to understand, perhaps, why it is important to make some changes if you want to give yourself the best possible chance of finding a happy and fulfilling relationship. And it is not just in that area that you will change because, as you know now, 'the way you do anything is the way you do everything' and so your whole life will improve. However unlikely that might seem to you at the moment, you can trust that it is a fact.

Before you begin the task of reinventing yourself though, it is important to recognise that some of the people who know you well might try to prevent this from happening. It is not that they are unpleasant or that they do not want the best for you; it is just that almost everybody resists change wherever it is in their life – it is an instinctive process linked to survival. You might just receive a few comments along the lines of: *"You've changed a lot lately,"* or perhaps: *"What on earth has come over you?"* It might even be something a bit stronger, like: *"You're getting a bit full of yourself, aren't you?"* It is best to make changes gradually, a little at a time, so that by the time anybody notices anything the process is well under way!

If you do encounter something like the above, though, the best response is a simple one: *"Well, yes, and it's working for me – and thank you for noticing!"* Said with a happy smile, this will disarm all but those who would be determined to 'keep you in your place' and you should not worry too much about what they think.

Getting started

The first step is a little time consuming but it is one that will pay huge dividends later on. At the top of a sheet of paper, write your name and the date, then the order of personality influences that are 'active' (one, two, or all three) with the major one first. Underneath that write: '**Positive resources:**' and a little way below that: '**Negative Resources:**' You will get something like this:

My Name, 11th February 2013. Settler, Nomad
Positive Resources:
Negative Resources:

Now study your major profile be it Warrior, Settler or Nomad, and pay special attention to the positive attributes there that seem to 'fit' you well. Write those down on your sheet. Look at the other profiles if they are relevant and write down the positive resources that you are sure truly apply to you.

Do the same exercise now with the negative resources, again only selecting those that you know are truly a part of you – **and do not be tempted to leave anything out.** Once that is done, write: '**Personality Style:'** and starting with the major profile, put down every part of the description that you are absolutely certain 'works' for you and, as before, do the same thing with the other personality styles if they are relevant. Write down everything that resonates with you, whether you view it as a good thing or a bad thing; if it is a part of you then it must be written down!

What you will have when you are finished will be totally unique. Recognise that this is the you that you are designed to be, the you that you truly deserve to be. The positive attributes can be strengthened by using them on a daily basis, while the negatives are destructive and need to be reined in, at least a little, when they start to make themselves felt. There are very few occasions indeed when they will achieve anything constructive.

Now think about a past relationship and imagine how it might have been different if you were this new person back there, back then. Imagine how you might have used those positive resources to deal with some of the difficulties that you encountered. It might be the case that it is already obvious to you that the relationship was not a good one, in which case think about how you would have decisively brought it to an end when it was time to do so, again using the positive resources associated with your profile. Do the exercise every day, using different situations if you wish, and make it as vivid as you can, because *anything you rehearse in your imagination will be far easier when you come to do it in real life.*

In the next chapter, we will set about the task of finding the best partner.

Chapter Three

The way people are and the games they play...

You have probably been told that you cannot judge a book by its cover... but you actually can and you actually do!

It is quite usual to like or dislike somebody as soon as you meet them, even though you may not realise why, and that is an instant assessment based on little more than the way they look – in other words, judging a book by its cover. Of course, later on, you might discover that your judgement was not very accurate and what you thought you were seeing was not actually what you were getting.

Right or wrong, the fact remains that you are used to making an assessment of somebody as soon as you meet them. You notice a great many things, in fact, including whether they are male or female, old or young, short or tall, and a whole pile of other stuff. It is a completely natural instinct and there is no reason on earth why you should stop doing it. There are many reasons, though, to learn how to make that snap decision as to what they are actually like as accurate as it can be. And that is what this chapter is about – quickly understanding somebody's personality type and knowing straight away if you are likely to be right for each other. Fortunately, that is actually much easier than you might think.

Each of the profiles shown later has an instant recognition guide that will allow you to quickly understand the personality of most people from the various clues that they give. Sometimes, it will not be immediately obvious but there will always be 'pointers' to help you. More than that, you will be able to see how a relationship with them would work when taking your own way of being into account. It is not foolproof because you can only see what somebody chooses to present to the world, not the *real* person inside... but it can still give you an astonishingly accurate idea of how they function.

The reason for such accuracy is that the 'way of being' of each type is deep-rooted and far older than you might realise, going all the way back to our ancient ancestors and the hostile world in which they lived. The behaviour patterns they adopted in order just to survive created those three 'colours' of personality:

- The **Warriors** had a chief who sought to control everything in their environment. Any personal softness would be viewed as a weakness that might threaten personal survival.

- The **Settlers** worked as a collective, with no single leader; they sought to understand their environment and always get the best out of it. Their strength was in numbers and they needed 'togetherness'. They formed the first human settlements.

- The **Nomads** were individuals who did what they wanted to do without worrying about others. The original renegades who disregarded any attempts to confine them, they were 'different from the crowd'.

These behaviour patterns became ingrained for hundreds of thousands of years, passed on from generation to generation in the DNA of their parents, and they are not about to disappear any time soon. Since civilisation started, though, some ten thousand years ago, there has been much interaction between different cultures and even races; nobody is a 'pure' representation of any one type any more although almost everybody will exhibit one of the three traits more strongly than the other two.

It is worth noting that an individual can easily be of a completely different personality from either parent. In truth, there is nothing remarkable about this, because genes often skip generations, so that an individual might be more like their grandparents or even their great-grandparents... or perhaps even a relative from a couple of centuries ago. All the more reason to start to be your 'real self' instead of how others thought you should be and tried to make you become!

While what you have been reading here will definitely help you to understand the type of person with whom you will be able to find happiness, there is more to be aware of and take into account. **Chemistry** for one thing. Although many relationships work successfully where that magical element is absent, there is always a risk that the missing ingredient will suddenly burst into your life and cause all kinds of havoc. You do not *have* to respond to it, though the urge to do so is certainly powerful. It will be easier to resist if what you already have is worthwhile – and only you will know if that is the case – and easier still if what you already have has its own chemistry.

The real risk comes when you are with somebody 'just because' – you and they were both available, sexually frustrated, did not find each other repellent and had enough opportunity to get together. You or they might never have intended it to become serious or permanent yet have somehow drifted into a partnership. That is when a sudden attack of chemistry with another can knock you off your feet!

Forewarned is forearmed, as they say, and if you can meet somebody who 'fits' what is right for you *and* fires up that magical component whenever you are together, you will be about as safe as it is possible to ever be in a relationship. It can feel like love, desire, admiration or something else entirely; the only thing that is certain is that it will fade over time. Not completely, perhaps, but enough that it becomes merely a part of the background. That is when you discover if what you have will stand the test of time. If it is right, then you and they will always want to be with each other more than with anybody else, and sharing your lives brings joy to both of you.

You already know something of each personality type from what you read in Chapter Two but now you are going to discover the finer details, some of which might surprise you. In fact, you will probably never look at anybody in the same way again, even the people that you thought you knew...

The first four aspects of each type – body language, speech, demeanour and dress – are listed in the order that is most likely to reveal the underlying personality.

Looking at... The Warrior

Body language: Usually fairly still with a steady gaze and certainly not expansive or expressive. Smiles are slight, often on one side of the face only, and sometimes the mouth may turn downwards in a smile instead of upwards.

Speech: Because they are not too concerned about what others think of them, there is often a habit of saying little and they will seldom find the need to explain themselves. Speech patterns do not usually show a great deal of expression unless anger or irritation is present.

Demeanour: Sensible and practical with a down-to-earth manner, the Warrior can also be very direct and sees little need for tact. They are often reserved, maybe even aloof, with people they do not know very well.

Dress: There is a liking for the darker colours like olive, navy, brown, with a tendency towards a conservative style. There is usually little in the way of jewellery or physical adornment and what there is is likely to be unfussy. Occasionally, females might dress more sharply, maybe in 'dramatic black' like some Nomads (see later). That can cause problems with recognition, but body language, speech and demeanour will reveal the truth.

Games they play: Warriors are by nature suspicious and testing, so will from time to time explore via mind games of various sorts to see if you are behaving yourself as they would like.

Extremes: At one end of the scale, they are calm and balanced, especially in an emergency; at the other end, you can find the bully who seeks to intimidate others into their bidding when things are not to their liking. Few individuals will show both extremes.

In relationships: This personality is not known for their warmth or emotional responses (except for anger or irritation) but is also not 'needy' or clinging. They are usually practically-minded, good at maintaining stability and tend to be uncompli-cated, though patience is sometimes lacking. They can be critical of others and sometimes accidentally upset those who have a gentler disposition, who may not realise that their bark is usually worse than their bite. They make good mates as long as there is little or no challenge to their need to be in charge and feel respected. In a good relationship, they will be supremely supportive of their partner and will always keep personal matters private. The need for control is always in evidence and admitting error is almost impossible for this type – this is not something they choose but a genetic trait from their ancestors, for whom being seen to be wrong could mean death.

Males tend to show all traits more strongly than **females,** who are usually more adaptable, though not necessarily less critical. Neither will be a 'cuddly' individual, though they do have their moments!

How it will work for you

If you are a **Warrior** yourself, then no matter what the second aspect is ('b' or 'c' in the personality test in the last chapter) this might not be a good relationship that will last. It could work reasonably well to begin with, as long as there is enough of that indefinable 'chemistry' at work, but with the passage of time it is likely to develop a destructive pattern. Neither you nor they will find it easy to give way in an argument – which is definitely necessary sometimes – and criticism of each other is almost inevitable. This is likely to lead to resentment which will destroy the closeness that is necessary if a relationship is going to remain rewarding and fulfilling. You are worth better, and better definitely *is* possible!

If you are a **Settler**, the strength of the Warrior will create a sense of security within you, while your own more adaptable nature will help to mediate the argumentative edge that you will definitely encounter. It will not be too much of a problem for you, since you are good at working with the feelings of others and will usually get the most positive best out of this personality type. They will be likely to appreciate your softness (though they may not show it very often) and your understanding nature, and will enjoy being in charge and looking after you, just as much as you enjoy your side of the deal. This combination can provide the ideal relationship for both, especially where you have 'a' and/or 'b' answers in your profile.

An exception might occur if you are a *total* Settler with a *total* Warrior, when you might well feel intimidated some of the time and worry about a lack of 'togetherness'. You will only discover this after a while, though, for it is quite difficult to assess the deeper part of an individual without getting to know them first.

TIP: If you start to feel intimidated or bullied, it probably will not improve no matter how long you wait or how hard you try.

If you are a **Nomad**, this *could* be a relationship made in Heaven! You will enjoy their strength and resolve, along with the ability to see things through and complete the tasks they start. You might find them a bit 'stuffy' on occasions and will not always get the sort of approval that you like but you will respect the way that their down-to-earth manner helps to keep you grounded. They, in turn, will find much pleasure in your light-heartedness and your ability to cheer them up when they are feeling low. All of this is particularly true if you have a 'b' in your profile.

There is an exception to this idyllic relationship and that is if you are with *total* Warrior and you are a *total* Nomad. Then, they will feel the need to somehow control your exuberance, which will lead to you feeling stifled and indignant at the restrictions they impose.

TIP: Once you feel like you want to escape in some way, it is probable that your Nomad ancestry has been triggered and it is time to move on. You might be able to make repairs if there is enough chemistry, though it will take a lot of determined effort.

Looking at... The Settler

Body language: Plenty of visual cues are given to show they are listening and understanding – nods, smiles and other facial expressions. Any dissent will usually produce a polite 'frost' rather than outright disagreement.

Speech: Like their demeanour, polite, pleasant and 'nice' with a tendency to explain themselves more than is necessary – they cannot abide to not be liked. Speech patterns are always conversational and agreeable.

Demeanour: Pleasant, 'nice', communicative and agreeable, with a non-judgemental attitude. Easy-going much of the time, they can change in an instant if something offends their sense of what is right and fair.

Dress: Mid-tone and pastel colours that blend and match rather than contrast. Severity and individuality are not part of this wardrobe and any jewellery will be conservative, rather than striking.

Games they play: The Settler is an expert at the 'silent martyr' mode when they are not getting what they want from a partner – even though they have not stated exactly what that is. It's often a case of: *"If you don't know, I'm not going to tell you..."*

Extremes: In positive style, this is a kind, loving and affectionate individual who will be a lover, parent, companion or nurse as necessary. The negative 'version' will show depression, moodiness, sulking and unhappy silence. Some individuals show both these extremes on occasions.

In relationships: The biggest problem with and for the Settler is their complexity. On the one hand they don't want to offend anybody because they cannot bear to be disliked, while on the other hand they usually have a rather lofty set of ideals that most people could not adhere to. When a partner transgresses one of their internal 'rules' there will not unusually be a somewhat frosty silence, and attempts to find out what is wrong will usually be met with a rather tight-lipped: *"Nothing."* Against this, they are genuinely forgiving and accepting of mistakes, though only when they are ready. Usually generous with all resources, they will give a lot of time to help others, even if it means foregoing some of their own plans. If this is questioned at any time, they will be mystified and hurt, not understanding why it should be thought that they would behave any differently. They love to share their lives and can become depressed, or sometimes irritated, if their partner seems not to appreciate this fact. The need for togetherness can result in apparent neediness and insecurity; it is not that they *cannot* manage on their own, though, just that they *do not want to.* This is possibly because of a genetically inherited subconscious belief that they are only safe when they are with others.

Females show these traits far more readily than do **males,** who are usually conditioned towards independence. Both are affectionate, enjoy physical contact, and are also naturally home-loving individuals.

How it will work for you

If you are yourself a **Settler,** then the lack of any form of threat of outrageousness coupled with the pleasant nature might well attract you to this mirror image of self. It *can* sometimes work but only rarely. It is easy to believe that your life would be full of love, companionship and understanding, and therefore rewarding. BUT there is an intrinsic need to be looked after and though it is a pleasantly romantic notion that you would look after each other, in practice it is rarely enough to deal with life's 'bombshell moments'. With this combination, there tends to be a growing recognition in both halves of the couple that something important is lacking, even if it cannot truly be defined, and it is almost inevitable that this will lead to a gradual drifting apart. Quite often, the relationship finally ends in sadness all round when one or the other meets somebody who 'hits the spot' squarely where it counts.

If you are a **Warrior,** especially with a 'b' in your profile, then this relationship can work quite well – eventually. It is unlikely that there will be much challenge to your need to be in control and you will certainly be nurtured and looked-after in life generally. It is a fact that you will be able to conduct the relationship almost exactly as you want to, as long as you are sure to observe the unwritten and unspoken 'rules' that you will have to discover by experience, which is where the weakness lies at the beginning. The Settler will do almost anything if you ask and almost nothing if you order or dictate, which can be frustrating for the Warrior individual. Get past this and you will have a loyal and loving partner who will tolerate your tendency to bossiness and love you all the more for it.

There is an exception here if you are a *total* Warrior (all 'a' answers in your profile). It is possible that you will unintentionally bully the Settler into compliance and then regard them as weak.

TIP: If you find yourself losing even the wish to respect this person as an equal in your life, it is probably time to set both of you free.

If you are a **Nomad,** especially with a 'b' in your profile, this relationship can work well, though it might lack some of the excitement and drama that you are inclined to seek. This is not a problem as long as you are able to fulfil this need in other areas of life, such as your work or hobbies. You will be sure to get the attention and fuss that you like, since the Settler will be impressed by your exuberance and optimism, even if they find it a little worrying at times. Because they are eager to please, you will usually discover that your sex life is as you want it to be; it is likely that this is very important to you so that is a big plus!

An exception occurs if you are a *total* Nomad, with all 'c' answers in your profile. Here your need for drama and excitement might well blind you to the fact that the Settler does not do drama very well at all. As a result they may become stressed and possibly depressed.

TIP: If you find yourself wondering why on earth your partner seems to be miserable a lot of the time, look closely at how you have been behaving. This is uncomfortable for you and if you cannot tolerate it, or don't wish to make any changes, the relationship might well have run its course.

Looking at... The Nomad

Body language: Obvious, as a rule, with exaggerated movements, face expressions and gesticulation. Emotionally-related responses such as shock, surprise, laughter, and everything else will be shown extremely clearly.

Speech: Animated and enthusiastic, quicker than the Warrior and more colourful than the Settler. Exaggeration is an art form with this type; large will be 'humongous', fast is 'a zillion miles an hour', unpleasant is 'gross' or maybe even 'totally gross' and so on.

Demeanour: Lively, enthusiastic and often exuberant, this type can sometimes be outrageous and usually has a great sense of occasion. They like to be 'different from the crowd' and enjoy being the centre of attention.

Dress: Almost always unusual in some way, even if not especially showy – though showy or colourful is not uncommon. Exceptionally smart or exceptionally scruffy, contrasting colours are often favoured; black with red, yellow, bright blue or green, mauve, for instance. Sometimes, there is a tendency for female Nomads to wear 'dramatic black'. Jewellery tends to be large and obvious. *Evident* 'style' is often important to the Nomad.

Games they play: There is a tendency to invent stories about extreme or unusual situations in order to impress others. They will do almost anything that guarantees attention and/or admiration.

Extremes: The extremes of 'Nomadness' are as far apart as it is possible to be, in many ways. At one end you have the inspiring, uplifting and genuinely charismatic individual, while at the other you find somebody who will try to cheat their way through life. Fortunately, though, the majority of Nomads are almost as responsible as the other two types and usually more fun.

In relationships: The main problem here is the constant need for attention and to be the centre of whatever is going on around them. A secondary issue is the extreme impatience at having to wait for *anything* – the need for instant gratification is a major 'trademark' of this personality. This extends into almost all areas of life, including sexuality. That apart, life with a Nomad is seldom tedious or boring; there is a liking for spontaneity that can sometimes become impulsiveness. Less serious than the Warrior and more outgoing than the Settler, they enjoy social-ising and are usually great entertainers. There is little in the way of complexity or depth with this individual and they are very much a 'what you see is what you get' personality. They can be generous and easy-going with money when the mood takes them, though when they are a 'bit short' this can lead to ill-advised borrowing to fund the latest whim or idea.

Males and **Females** show these traits fairly equally, particu-larly when young, though females are often more colourful in their appearance. Both are likely to seek to outdo others around them, especially on the dance floor, at work, or in a social gathering.

How it will work for you

If you are a **Nomad** yourself, with or without any 'a' or 'b' answers in your profile, a relationship with this individual is likely to prove very difficult for both of you. You might well be hugely attracted to this fun-loving soul but it is likely that there will be an almost constant vying for attention which will result in the: *"What about me?"* and: *"How do you think that makes me feel?"* type of argument. Because you *need* attention – and this is not in any way a criticism, for you didn't choose the way you 'work' – you won't always be very good at giving it unless there's something in it for you. But your partner would probably be exactly the same and therefore also not good at being attentive to your needs. Eventually a fair amount of resentment can develop, along with feelings of not being appreciated, and it is probably obvious to you that this is a dangerous situation as far as sustaining a happy relationship is concerned. Sexual attraction is often high at the beginning, along with mutually ecstatic activity but if that is the only thing you share, your journey through life together is likely to be a rather short one.

If you are a **Settler** then you can be completely swept off your feet by the sheer exuberance and enthusiasm with which this personality type embraces life. It is as if a breath of fresh air has found its way into your usually-responsible existence and you can feel as if you have truly 'come alive' for the first time in your life. If you have a 'c' in your profile, then you might well be able to sustain this relationship for a lifetime, though there will be occasions where it seems to be hard work and you feel as you are having to behave as a parent to a child. It will depend on you being able to provide some stability while at the same time enjoying the unpredictability of this sometimes erratic and hopelessly optimistic individual. It will always be a comple-mentary partnership, each of you possessing attributes that the other does not have – but this can actually work extremely well.

There is an exception here if you have an 'a' in your profile and are with a Nomad who tends to cheat their way through all manner of situations. Then, your irritation will eventually reach damaging proportions.

TIP: If you begin to discover that even tiny things irritate you to the point of exasperation, don't wait for things to improve. They won't. You don't handle irresponsibility at all well and you will eventually succumb to anger and a complete lack of respect. At that point, of course, it is finished.

If you are a **Warrior**, especially with 'a' or 'b' answers in your profile, this type of personality can be a near-perfect partner. It works slightly better with the combination of Warrior male and Nomad female, though it can still be excellent when it is the other way round. There is a tiny downside in that you will be expected to be more demonstrative than is usually the case for you, though the sheer light-heartedness of this individual can easily inspire you to behaviour that some others would perceive as 'out of character' – if you let it, that is, and as long as you do not think too hard about it. The rewards are high; you will have a ray of light into your previously rather serious existence and you will provide a rock of stability for somebody who might never have felt so secure at any time. There is no doubt that you would be respected in such a relationship, which is important to you, and all you would have to give in return is the occasional assurance that you were impressed! You probably would be, too.

The exception here is if you are a *total* Warrior (all 'a' answers) with an excessively exuberant Nomad, especially one who cheats. Your instinctive urge will be to attempt to control this individual, a fruitless and almost impossible task. Frustration, stress and resentment on both sides will eventually finish the whole thing off.

TIP: If what once seemed like a love story without equal begins to feel like a burden of responsibility and frustration, the time has come to free both of you from what will eventually become an emotional prison.

Bent but not broken...

If you are in a relationship which is a bit 'rocky' but not really broken, you have a chance to make it stronger via a new understanding and acceptance of how you and your partner truly work. You can see both of you in a new light, perhaps, now that you are able to identify the underlying personality of each of you. For many people, just recognising *why* they or somebody else is behaving in a certain way is enough to make huge improvement possible.

For instance, a Warrior personality does not *choose* to see the downside of things; it is an inherited instinct. Their ancestors would not have survived had they not have observed what might go wrong and taken steps to avoid it. The upside is that they also have an inherited ability to find resources that will provide answers to problems, something their ancient relatives had to do if they were to stay alive. That is why being right is so important to the Warrior; making a wrong decision is linked to survival fears.

Whatever a partner does or does not do is not aimed at you, even if it feels like it – that's just your own reaction based on your own instincts – it's simply an expression of the way they actually *are*. It's even possible, with what you have learnt here, to help them to find and use their positive resources effectively. After all, they might well not be properly aware of their skills and strengths, only their weaknesses.

The individual profile that you created for yourself can help you greatly here; study it all closely and look at what really works in the relationship and what is either unfulfilled or gets in the way. Change what you can and accept what you cannot, and if there is something that you have to accept but which is in some way undesirable, control it with all your might. You can only create change within yourself, not your partner, though you might be able to help them find a different way of being if they truly want to.

If all of this seems just too much like hard work, then you might need to read **Chapter Eleven:** *When it all goes wrong,* and **Chapter Fourteen:** *A trick or two to deal with a break up...*

Starting over again

If you are in the 'wanting to find someone' situation at the moment, then you are reading this at exactly the right time! Practise using the positive aspects of your profile on a daily basis, whatever they are, because this will strengthen them and make them more natural. You only really need to work at one of them at a time, because as you know now, the way you do anything is the way you do everything. Strengthen one attribute and you are enhancing the rest so choose one that you feel comfortable working with. Look at the entire description each evening and make a note of which parts were active that day; after a while, you will begin to notice if something appears to be left out and you can begin to work on it.

It's a good idea to study the people around you at every opportunity – those you work with and those you see at the bus stop, in shops, at the pub, cafe, or anywhere else you go, and practise recognising what personality group they belong to. After a while, this can become second nature and almost as simple as noticing the colour of their hair or how tall they are. Friends, relatives, and others you have known for a long time can often seem difficult to 'do' at first, because it is easy to be swayed by what you *think* you know about them. Be guided by what you have read in this chapter though, and keep an open mind, and you will be amazed at what you can suddenly understand about why they are the way they are.

Chapter Four

Something old, something new

Finding a new mate and making the relationship work can be much easier than many people think. One of the most important aspects is to recognise that it is a new situation. It's totally unique, not simply a replay of something that has gone before. That new understanding is especially vital now, after what you have read so far about avoiding the 'same old, same old'.

It's likely that if you are already with someone, you might think that this chapter has little to offer but you would be wrong about that for a very simple reason. Many, if not most, people will continue to stay with a partner for ages after it has become obvious that the time has come to part. The idea of starting all over again is daunting and perhaps the worst part of it is the fear of being alone, maybe even forever. But if they *knew beyond doubt* that they were soon to find someone new, or even only that it would not be too difficult to do so, then they would make the break a lot earlier and with less sadness all round. There are obviously other factors to be taken into account, such as somewhere to live, joint friends, possessions and so on; yet these things suddenly seem to be far less important the very instant somebody new comes on the scene.

Something old...
Your history of partnerships, whether they have been long-lasting affairs, brief 'flings', marriage, living together or anything else is far more important than you might realise. This is especially true if it involves hurt and recrimination, physical or emotional abuse, cheating by either half, failure to talk, too many sexual difficulties, continual arguments, criticism, or any of the other negative concepts that are all too common. The experience

of those things can lead you to believe that relationships just do not work for you and may well have you expecting more of the same. And because you usually manage to find exactly what you look for, it might even be the reason you have found more of the same in the past!

It's important to remember it's all just part of what has gone and not part of who you are or what you do. There is absolutely no reason to imagine that how you felt – and how you behaved as a result – with a previous partner will be exactly the same when you are with somebody else whose 'way of being' is different. Unless you try, albeit subconsciously, to make it so...

The problem is that even if you do your very best to keep an open mind, you can still be biased, still looking for what you might believe is the inevitable, unless you manage to turn things on their head a little.

It's not a lot better when your history is full of joy, love and shared togetherness; then you could spend an awful long time searching for a replacement that will slot seamlessly into your life. Here, though, you are likely to subscribe to that old *"I'll never find anyone like that ever again..."* concept – and if you keep on telling yourself so, that will definitely be the case! You will always look for, and eventually find, evidence that any new partner is simply not entitled to inhabit the pedestal you have built for them...

There is one other possibility; you know about misery and hurt and constantly search for the something better that you know is 'out there'. Well, you almost certainly can find it, as long as what you are looking for is realistic. The one common denominator in all your relationships is **you**. Everybody you meet is the unique product of thousands upon thousands of years of culture, traditions and personal family history being passed from one generation to the next... which means that every individual is different. Just like you. The underlying personality is easy to spot; the way it is expressed is a markedly different kettle of fish indeed! So if it always seems to end up going the same way, it is odds-on that you have something to do with it! This is a good thing, because it gives you a chance to work directly at the problem.

It's important to recognise that every relationship is a brand new and exciting adventure and it is entirely up to you whether you seek to discover what there is in it that's wonderful, or look for what you hope is not there but fear you might find anyway.

Something new...

After the last chapter you have some idea of the sort of person you are most likely to find happiness with. It's worth noting that if you feel that this is the sort of person you have been with before, then you are more than half-way to success; you already know how to recognise this sort of individual and all you have to do now is discover how to make it work properly next time – and there is more about that later on in this book.

It's important to be totally realistic; forget those wonderful lives you sometimes see in films and on television because they are based on what the screenwriters know most people would love to find. This is the myth:

- The men are successful
- The women always have their 'face' on, whatever the time of day
- The men are thoughtful, fair and good-humoured
- The women juggle a great job and a perfect home
- Both halves of a couple are communicative and supportive
- There is always something interesting happening
- They have great friends who are always helpful when it is needed

The 'real world' is different though. Men have difficulties in their career; friends are sometimes just not available and people are occasionally irritated with each other for no good reason. Life often becomes boring, women's make-up goes shiny, and all manner of uncomfortable things attempt to wreak havoc from time to time via a 'cosmic conspiracy' that seems to have a grandly ironic sense of timing.

The happy fact is that none of these is truly important in the great scheme of things, unless you make it so. They will always be part of every relationship and just the simple act of recognising that they *are* an actual part of the relationship makes them far easier to cope with. They are affecting both halves of the couple. They are normal and they are certainly not permanent. What is more, if you are with the right partner, you will both weather the mini storm and come out the other side smiling as if nothing much had happened.

The only predictable truth is that you cannot possibly know how things will work out with a new somebody until you try it. If you like it, you can do your best to nurture it with what you read here. If it just does not work for the 'real you' then you know that it is time to quit before things get too involved.

Of course, you first have to find that new somebody...

In the beginning

If you are a supremely confident person you might already find meeting new people and forming new relationships to be a simple matter, although you will still benefit from what is written here. But if you tend to lack confidence, especially with the 'opposite sex', then you are about to get a real boost!

More people meet a potential mate at work than in any other single situation but this only means that it is convenient, not that it is ideal. It's easy to imagine that the joint interest can make for greater closeness but it is a fact that most people's work 'persona' is somewhat different from their social self, and different again from their romantic or sexual self. It does not mean it cannot work, only that what attracts you at first might be only a 'work front' that is completely lacking in other areas of life. It needs thinking about. Also, there can be an uncomfortable situation if you break up, and there's no answer for that. It's one of the downsides of meeting people in this way.

*If a workmate fascinates you, be sure that they **really** 'turn you on' and it's not just based on the fact that you and they are both available. Ask yourself if you would feel the same if you met them in a totally different situation. If not, then it might still work but equally, you might be just wasting your time and missing the chance of meeting somebody else. Convenience is not really a very good reason for choosing a mate!*

In social situations, there is a different set of problems, because for so many people, making the first approach is fraught with anxiety and fear of rejection. There is also the screamingly embarrassing hiatus when, having made some sort of contact, you have to wait to see what sort of response you are going to get. Even more than that, finding some way to exit the situation with dignity when it did not work out well is not an easy task. For these reasons, many people – females as well as males – often just look longingly at somebody, wondering, wishing, and hoping for some sort of miracle to happen.

It does not have to be like that, fortunately. Though the approach for males differs a little from that for females and also for the personality of the person you are trying to get to know, it is quite easy to avoid all that awkwardness. Imagine, just for a moment, that you have laid eyes on somebody you really like the look of. The first thing is to assess whether they appear to be the right personality for you, using the information from **Chapter Three.** This is actually very important, because when we find somebody sexually attractive, the heady combination of chemistry, body scent and physical looks can easily lead us astray. These things are obviously enormously important in a relationship but if they are coupled with the 'wrong' personality it can be a recipe for confusion and disaster. If they are coupled with the 'right' type, though, something wonderful is possible.

There is actually another consideration, one that is occasionally unpalatable to some, and that is social class. This needs to be taken into account but we will not go into that particularly 'prickly' subject here – most people are already very well aware of the difficulties that can arise from a mismatch in that area. So we will assume that this person who is firing your buttons seems to be 'suitable' and we can now have a look at how you can approach them without feeling awkward, and without having to worry about an outright rejection – in fact an outright rejection simply cannot happen if you follow this plan.

For the male

Study the female you would like to get to know and decide what it is about her physically that attracts you most – this is essential if you are to appear sincere when you make your approach. Now, this is vital; to avoid the risk of offending her, only choose from these areas: **eyes; nose; hair; ears; shoulders** (if they are bare).

Shortly, when you have gathered enough confidence, you are going to walk close by her, apparently on your way to somewhere else – it is not important where, particularly, as long as you can go there and return a couple of minutes later. As you pass by, pause for just long enough to make eye contact and speak to her, though what you say will depend on what personality she appears to be. 'Eyes' is used for an example here:

- **Warrior:** *"I hope I don't offend you but you really do have the most beautiful eyes...."*
- **Settler:** *"I hope I don't embarrass you – but I've just got to tell you that you really do have absolutely beautiful eyes..."*
- **Nomad:** *"I've really **got** to tell you that you have **the most** astonishingly beautiful and sexy eyes! You look absolutely stunning!"*

If you don't feel confident enough to say all that, you can pause just long enough to say: *"You've got really beautiful eyes,"* with a tone of voice that suits the personality – calm, with the emphasis on *"really"* for the Warrior, gentle, with the emphasis on *"beautiful"*, for the Settler and enthusiastic, with the emphasis on *"You've"*, for the Nomad. Now just walk on, and be sure not to wreck everything by looking back. Wherever you go, return around two minutes later. If when you first spoke to her, she wished that she was anywhere but there, she will now be anywhere but there... On the other hand, if she has not moved away, you can be reasonably certain that she liked you too. What happens next is up to you and the only big mistake you could make would be to ignore her. Smiling is good. If you are in the right setting, asking if you can buy her a drink is good.

It's not a perfect approach and some will probably see it as 'cheesy' or worse. But it does at least remove all sorts of awkwardness from that first encounter, and the knowledge that you don't have to wait for a response can provide a huge boost to your confidence.

Some males worry greatly that any female they talk to will know straight away what is *really* in their mind, which at the most basic level is sex. That is, after all, why one person seeks to get to know another. Well, you can relax. She *will* know straight away and if she responds to your attention in any positive manner at all, then this is a very good sign indeed! As an example, you might ask her if you can buy her a drink and she will translate that as: *"I'd like to have sex with you."* If she says: *"Thank you! I'll have a glass of wine..."* (or whatever) you can interpret that as: *"If you behave yourself, I might let you..."*

For the female

In general, males are extremely likely to respond positively to a female who makes an advance towards them but there are two important things to be aware of:

- He will **want** to like you and try his hardest to do so; his sexual instinct is such that if he thinks it is on offer (it's inevitable that he will) he will not want to pass up the opportunity
- Don't be obvious in front of his mates – they will 'take the mickey' out of him later on and he will know it. This might discourage him from responding positively

The actual approach is easy and exactly the same as for the male – pass close by, speak, and walk on without looking back. You can choose just about anything to use as a compliment as long as you feel comfortable saying it. This will include his clothes, shoulders, waist, bottom (though you would refer to it as 'bum'), hair, hands or almost anything else that can decently be spoken of in public. His personality type is important too if your compliment is going to have maximum effect:

- **Warrior:** Be brief and not too personal. There is no need to actually pause as you pass by but do try to make eye contact and quietly say something like: *"Nice hands..."* or: *"Your hair's great..."* Brevity is best with this one and it will intrigue him.
- **Settler:** The main thing here is not to be either dramatic or too brief; the first might embarrass him while the second might leave him uncertain as to whether you are genuinely interested in him. Make eye contact and say something like: *"You know, you really do have nice hands..."* or: *"I really like the way your hair looks..."*
- **Nomad:** It's actually difficult to get it wrong with the male Nomad! As soon as you say anything to him he will assume you fancy him and mischievous brevity is best here: *"Nice bum!"* as you walk past will almost certainly work, as also will: *"Phwoar!"* followed with a slight laugh.

When you return from wherever you walk to, the same 'rules' as for the male apply; if he's still there, you have scored a hit, but if he has disappeared, or turned his back to where you must pass by, you shouldn't waste time looking for him. He has turned away from an apparently willing female – and that is pretty final!

Sometimes, a male will instantly follow you, especially a Nomad type, maybe claiming that he did not quite hear what you said. Well, whether he did or did not, he likes you; no man will pursue a female that he finds unattractive and now he is exhibiting anxiety that you might get away. To put it rather bluntly, whether he has waited for you or followed you, you now have him hooked and it is up to you what happens next. And when.

Meeting places

For many, actually meeting new people, never mind whether or not they are available or attractive, poses the greatest difficulty. You might feel that the club/pub scene just doesn't suit you any more, even if it did in the first place. Perhaps experience has taught you to be very wary of a blind date with those who have a 'lovely personality' and you have also discovered that the individuals on the free internet dating sites post photographs that are twenty years out-of-date, have optimistic scales and tape measures, and so frequently are not 'on the same wavelength' as you. Not on the same wavelength as most, in fact.

It *can* be difficult, there is no doubt about that, but there are agencies that take a great deal of care with the 'vetting' of their members. Generally, the more questions they ask to discover compatible matches, the better they are and the more they will deter the thrill seekers and the married-and-only-in-search-of-sex type of individual. There are many people who meet a partner that way and it could work for you, too. Maybe it will not be the first introduction, nor perhaps the second, but it can certainly happen. It's a lot better than waiting forlornly for the universe to work some sort of miracle for you.

An alternative is to join some activity or other, ideally one that interests you, since it will also attract people with whom you are likely to at least feel you have something in common. Here are a few ideas, in no particular order:

Camera clubs; art classes; sailing clubs; rambling associations; gymnasia; writers circles; meditation groups; dance classes; martial arts classes; language classes; cookery classes; DIY classes; adult education; evening classes in loads of subjects, and more.

A reminder

Although these two points have been mentioned earlier in the book, they are worth repeating, especially in relation to finding a new mate.

- Be sure to look for the one that you want to be with, rather than somebody who you think others would approve of.
- Right from the start, be the real you that you might have only recently discovered. You can never sustain an act for a lifetime.

That last point is of enormous importance since it can be very tempting to adopt a certain stance or style that you know your potential new mate is looking for and yet is not really you. If you succeed in your sales pitch, you will have attracted someone who is not really suitable for you. That really is a case of false pretences and might just lead to more of the same old, same old...

Chapter Five

What the other half doesn't know...
about sex

It's important to understand that much of this chapter is about the **biology** *behind the sexual attitudes and behavior patterns of men and women. It therefore initially ignores such concepts as equality and women's rights – neither of which existed when our sexual 'roots' were created. If they had, the notion of creating them wouldn't have been needed. Also, the behaviours outlined here are generalised and while they will be accurate for most, it is entirely possible that some of them may not apply to you.*

An old man once said: *"It ain't what you know that causes a problem and it ain't what you don't know that causes a problem. It's what you don't know but think you do that causes all the difficulties in life."* This was never as true as it is in people's sex lives!

Sex is such an important part of a relationship that this chapter and the next are dedicated to that particular subject. We're not talking about knowing or not knowing techniques here – that is actually the easiest part of sexual activity – but of understanding your partner's thought processes. It's then that 'what you don't know but think you do' can cause all sorts of difficulties. Much of the problem stems from the natural tendency to assume that what another person says or does means exactly the same as it would if you did it. We will look at that idea and how it applies to sexual behaviour later on but first it's important to recognise an extraordinarily simple truth: men and women have totally different attitudes in life generally. You are probably already aware of this but it's almost certainly the case that you do not fully understand exactly *why* they should be so different, or even how different they are!

It's all to do with instinctive behaviour inherited from our ancestors of almost two hundred thousand years ago, the nomadic hunter-gatherers, and maybe even earlier. The most important thing back then was simply to survive and males and females had totally different tasks in that respect. As far as we know today, the males, being more heavily built, were the hunters and warriors, while the females were the gatherers of fruits and roots and so on. In addition, the males had to do battle to defend their people from other tribes and the females had to rear the young and tend to the older members of their group.

Male survival was based on destruction; female survival was based on nurture.

It's difficult to imagine that those processes could be any more different from each other! Even though the beginnings of civilisation some 10,000 years ago subtly changed the nature of our existence, we still carry the instinctive urges that eventually became 'born in' to our more distant relatives. This shows in the goal-orientated approach of many males and the multi-tasking abilities of most females. Hunting, fighting and killing demanded a single-minded and goal-orientated approach, while nurturing offspring and each other needed flexibility and an ability to perform several tasks at the same time. Of course, these days, there are target-orientated females and nurturing, multi-tasking males but this is the exception rather than the rule. For most, the old instincts are still active.

Another behaviour pattern that is related to those far-off days shows up quite strongly in same-sex group behaviour. In general, females tend to share each others' *company*, just as their ancient relatives might have done in the tribal encampment – think modern day 'coffee mornings'. Males, again in general, share each others' *environment* in the same way that the tribesmen might have done in battle – and think football matches in the modern day. Women will converse more and about a wide range of subjects; men will converse mostly about the subject at hand.

You might already be starting to recognise, by now, that the instinctive differences between men and women are so great that it's hardly a surprise that there's frequently a high degree of misunderstanding. But the processes of each, in the early days of humanity, performed equally important tasks of survival. So if something about the way that the 'opposite sex' behaves irritates you at some point, reflect upon the fact that it's all to do with what they inherited from their distant relatives. Without it you probably would not have even been here to grumble about it!

The 'understanding gap' is most profound in matters of sexuality, since this is where there is the greatest conflict of all. Males and females have always had to have – and still do have – totally different sexual responses, many of them associated with survival as you will see later on. They form a fundamental behaviour pattern, ingrained over hundreds of thousands of years, that's almost impossible to change without potentially causing all sorts of problems, including threats to physical and emotional health. That might sound extreme but it's a fact that seeking to inhibit natural responses can lead to all manner of psychosexual dysfunction, including impotence in males and vaginismus (a painful spasm of the vaginal muscles) in females on any attempt at sexual intercourse.

Now, before you read on, remember that what's written here is purely about the inherited instinctive sexual behaviour associated with males and females of the human species. It takes no account of 'higher values', morals, sophistication or equality and is only intended to enlighten you as to the origins of some of the most frustrating attitudes that can be encountered in a partner. It seeks to remain objective though you might well decide, whether you are male or female, that it's actually making excuses for the behaviour of one or the other. If so, then just remember that we are talking about the very reason for your existence and quite possibly also the reason for your difficulties in relationships.

Understanding and seeking to accept will serve you much better in your future than will resistance and trying to reject!

The honeymoon period

None of us, male or female, are designed to stay with one sexual partner for the whole of our lifetime, even though it does happen that a couple remain blissfully happy for a half-century or more. Those people are indeed fortunate and will often feel that they have found their 'soul mate'. And perhaps they have. They are not typical, though, since we actually do not have the pair-bonding gene that naturally monogamous animals, such as swans, possess. The closest we get to it is during the sexual act when we receive a shot of a hormone called *oxytocin* (often referred to as the 'love hormone') which is known to increase feelings of love and closeness. For the rest of the time we are at the mercy of the very attribute which has led to our existence, the drive to produce offspring by as many different partners as possible to ensure that at least some of them will survive. The 'honeymoon period', when we do not even want to look at anybody else lasts, for most people, around six months or so. After that, there is a little while when we might look but have no wish to pursue the idea of sexual contact, and finally, after a total period of about two years, we will begin to find certain other people sexually attractive. That is not to say that we will do anything about it. Many do not, instead settling for the security of familiarity, as long as the relationship is at least tolerable. But the fact remains that they will look at others and maybe fantasise about them.

This is not something we choose to do nor is it anything that we can voluntarily suspend. It's an inherited instinct, as is so much of our sexual behaviour, and although many people do manage to control it, for others it proves to be an impossible task. We cannot control what we feel, only what we *do with* what we feel. Personality comes into this process and we will examine how that works later in this chapter.

In one particular respect, the human animal is no different from any other – the female has something that the male desperately wants and he will chase it incessantly. He will fight for it, plead for it, beg for it, scheme for it and all but die for it. He has a kind of built in radar that will alert him to the presence of a sexually viable female even on the rare occasions when he is not consciously searching for one. This drive is so intense that it can easily override common sense and responsibility and the only surprising thing is that he frequently manages to control the urges that arise from it. An interesting prospect is that where some think that females are being exploited (as in 'Page Three Girls') it's easy to imagine that it might actually be the male's sex drive that is being exploited by the publishers!

It's not only the male who exhibits a deeply instinctive behaviour associated with sex, though. The truth is that he also has something that the female wants and which she will pursue avidly, though it has to be said with probably less intensity than the male exhibits in his pursuit of sex. That something is money, the modern representation of the hunter's spoils. Distasteful as it might be to some, this is a totally natural response, though a female might not be *consciously* aware that it's operative while she's seeking a mate. The most successful male was the one who could provide the greatest level of security (which is what money does these days, of course) for the female, her children and the tribe in general. For that very reason, successful males were and still are highly attractive to most females and just as he has a radar system to alert him to a sexually attractive female, so she has a similar awareness of a desirable male. She knows about the intensity of his sex drive and will use it as a hook on which she places herself as bait, just as her ancient relatives did, and he never, ever, minds!

Some or all of the last two paragraphs might be irritating or downright offensive to many – but remember that we are talking about the biological background that has contributed to the outrageous success of the human race, as far as survival is concerned.

None of this is to say that we must or should allow ourselves or our partner to be unfaithful, just that it stems from a deeply ingrained instinct. Infidelity is intensely painful and if we ever wanted to be with a partner in the first place, they deserve our respect and consideration when we no longer wish to stay. That last bit, about respect and consideration, is not an ancient concept; in fact it's very modern, which might be the reason why so many find it difficult to implement – it's not based on instinctive urges, so conscious thought, guilt, embarrassment and sometimes sheer cussedness get in the way.

The major difference

All of this can translate down to some pretty fundamental differences in behaviour, the most noticeable of which is in the immediacy of response. The very instant a 'normal' man sees a female, no matter what he is doing, he knows whether or not he would have sex with her, without having to think about it or consider any consequences. He is designed that way and has no choice in the matter. The process cannot be voluntarily stopped any more than noticing the colour of somebody's hair can be stopped. It's not something he has any control over and is an integral part of maleness. If it stops, it means something is wrong.

Females function in a totally different way, though, which can lead to some very odd circumstances on occasions, especially when in an established relationship. Much of the time, she might not even be thinking about perhaps later on allowing herself to be aroused into sexual desire. She is in what can be thought of as a 'buffer zone' that sits between her day-to-day tasks and her sexual self. Males usually have no idea of this concept, any more than females are aware of the inability of the male to 'switch off' the sexual hunting instinct. If he smiles at a female, she, being in the buffer zone, might think what a pleasant fellow he is and smile back; he, being in the hunting mode, assumes this to be a favourable response to a perceived sexual advance. He might not do anything about it but will perceive that he could have done so. She, though, might have no idea that there was any sexual play of any sort whatsoever.

This brings us to the basics of the first of several misunderstandings within a relationship:

- The male sex drive is constantly active and cannot be turned off by choice. It's not disrespectful, an indicator of excessive demands, or in some way disgusting. It's just a facet of maleness.
- The female sex drive is usually on standby though can be turned on relatively easily... but only if the circumstances are right. The lack of instant desire is not an indicator of frigidity or lack of interest, just a facet of femaleness.

Neither response is 'better', more mature or more desirable, since they are both associated with a process that is totally natural for their gender but they can each cause annoyance and unfounded accusations from their partner. There is another circumstance, closely related, that also causes difficulty. The male has always had to hunt and the most successful sexual hunters with the greatest sense of urgency necessarily produced the highest number of children. Those offspring would inherit that high drive and pass it on to *their* children... and so it continues. It's the same in just about all animals and you can see that it's closely associated with survival of the species, if you think about it. If you have ten females and one male, the population can grow quite quickly. If you have ten males and one female, it will grow very slowly if at all.

The male carries the possibility of producing three hundred and sixty five children a year, so a missed chance is one less member of the species. No wonder he might get angry when sex

has been half-promised but then withheld for whatever reason...
For the female it's really only one child a year, so her 'window of
opportunity' is quite wide and one missed incidence of sexual
intercourse is of no great consequence. So no wonder she is
nowhere nearly as concerned as the male. Obviously, no
individual thinks in those terms – it's pure instinct, inherited
from those who were most likely to keep tribal numbers replen-
ished. The ones who got most angry and frustrated if they missed
out were driven more to pursue it. The female, on the other hand,
never did have to hunt because it always came to her and that
much is still the same. And because of these differences between
male and female responses we can now begin to see another
potential trouble area in most relationships:

- Women will never be able to truly understand the
  relentless sensation of urgency that the male has inherited
  and she might wrongly interpret it as selfishness. His
  frustration can rise to unbearable levels if an encounter
  fails or is missed completely, especially if she has given
  him the impression she wants to do it.
- Men will never be able to truly understand the female's
  need for a longer period of arousal and might wrongly
  interpret it as a lack of interest. This is compounded by the
  fact that most women are far more tolerant of a failed or
  missed encounter than the male is able to be.

This particular difference in attitudes accounts for the way that a
male who is a perfectly reasonable individual in the normal way
suddenly transforms into a scowling, vehement lout when
denied sex for any reason at all. This is actually extremely
counter-productive, in that it may well serve to convince his
partner that that was all he was interested in, anyway. She is just
a vagina, rather than a valued partner. Not a surprise, then, that
she might become irritated and unwilling when he wants to do it

the next day... or maybe compliant, but unenthusiastic. Unfortunately, the male interprets this perfectly understandable response as if it means what it would if *he* were behaving the same way: *"She's punishing me."* Then, thanks to the fragility of the male sexual ego, something rather odd happens; he begins to fear that she no longer loves him.

This response might seem extreme to his partner, especially since it was his bad manners that caused her coolness in the first place, but there is a sound reason for it. It's not a revelation, of course, that a male can quite easily have sex with somebody he finds desirable but does not love, just as a female can. But while a female can love a man without necessarily wanting to have sex, this is simply not the case for the male. He cannot love his partner without wanting to have sex with her. So the more it seems to him that she does not want to do it, the more he believes that it's possible, even likely, that she is falling out of love with him – or maybe doing it with somebody else. Just as it's completely incomprehensible to him that his partner can enjoy sexual intercourse without necessarily achieving orgasm, so it's as difficult for him to believe that she can truly love him without wanting sex. To the male, love must *always* engender sexual desire. To put it rather bluntly:

- If his penis is being rejected he will feel that *he* is being rejected.
- If she feels that he is only interested in her vagina, she will feel that that is all she is as far as he is concerned.

Each of those states is every bit as uncomfortable as the other and it's easy to see why severe problems in the relationship can arise as a result.

Sexual insecurity

A lack of communication about the sort of situations outlined above can quickly lead to sexual insecurity, something that men tend to suffer far more frequently than do women. Males are acutely aware that in our modern life they cannot necessarily follow those inherited instincts for frequent sexual activity if their partners do not want to, and yet it's a psychologically essential part of their behaviour. Without it, there is a subconscious belief that he is not fulfilling his biological obligations – he is not replenishing the tribe. The subconscious neither knows nor cares about family planning, birth control, or any other limitation. As far as he is concerned, if he is sometimes ejaculating inside a female, even while wearing a condom, everything is just as it should be; if not, then he is not behaving like a 'proper man', a subconscious process that can sometimes lead to quite severe depression.

Remember, we are not talking about the rights and wrongs of relationships here but simply about biologically inherited instincts which are at the root of male behaviour.

Women tend to be less prone to sexual insecurity for two reasons: firstly, the instinctive immediate need tends to be lower, as mentioned earlier, and secondly it's far easier in general for a woman to get sexual activity when she wants to, especially within a workable relationship. She doesn't have to wonder if it will happen, doesn't have to worry about it, since she is actually pretty much in charge of whether it does or not. She can actually decide that she will have sex and be reasonably confident that she will not be rejected. For the male, that would be Utopia! He will eventually lose count of the number of times that he has been completely preoccupied about whether he will 'get lucky' or not.

His sexual insecurity manifests itself in many ways, two of which are immensely irritating to women:

1 'Pawing and grabbing' at every opportunity
2 Constant 'going on' about his desperate need

What most males never quite 'get' is that neither of these behaviours will produce the result they are seeking, which is willingness or better still, eagerness, on the part of their partner. They are actually far more likely to have completely the opposite effect, associating discomfort and criticism with sexual activity. In addition to this, the amount of psychological pressure that this applies to the female will make it almost impossible for her to respond in a loving way. It has become a battle and the feeling of 'giving in' is hardly conducive to passionate love-making.

On the other hand, what most females seldom 'get' is the fact that while he is irritating her by his ceaseless nagging, protesting and maybe sly remarks, he definitely wants sex *with her*. Not with anybody else. He is going about it all the wrong way but there is no doubt that this is what he wants. Not only that, when he goes on about it at length, it's usually because it just is not happening at all. She might complain that he wants to do it all the time – and it will certainly feel like it – where the reality is that he just wants to do it *once*, without even pondering on the next time. By the time it has got to this stage, though, it's likely that there are other problems in the relationship anyway.

The only answer here is something for which women have a natural instinct but which is an alien concept as far as most males are concerned – conversation. And therein lies another problem. If a woman talks with her partner about their sex life, she is trying to improve it in the future. Meanwhile, the male is happy enough to talk about it but thanks to the immediacy response, he wants to do it *now!* This situation has the potential to cause huge arguments, convincing the female that he *was* only interested in sex all along, and leaving the male certain that she was criticising him for wanting her.

One of the situations that can so easily create this type of misunderstanding is what can be referred to as the 'interpretation of intent'. As soon as a female gets the idea that sex is actually *expected* for whatever reason, she might well feel as if she is just a chattel, something that he believes he 'owns' in some way. A typical scenario is where a couple have been out for a meal, say; they have been to a great restaurant, have had wonderful food and good wine, as well as an evening of togetherness and he is now feeling in an amorous mood. At this point, they both make a mistake. He becomes eager to get home and she interprets this as an evidence of his expectation. In fact, for the vast majority of males, it's actually *hope* they are experiencing. it's almost certain that it was in his mind from the beginning and just as likely that it was in her mind, too, but his over-eagerness and her misinterpretation has spoiled the whole thing.

All of what you are reading here is likely to be familiar to you and it's to be hoped that whether you are male or female, you are now beginning to gain a more positive understanding of why the 'opposite sex' can be so infuriating without meaning to be! And that is very important: **without meaning to be.** Of course, communication is the answer and there is a lot of help for that later on in the book.

The act...

Now we come to the area where there is probably the highest number of misconceptions of all... the actual act of sex itself. This is not just about sexual intercourse but about the whole process of before, during and after. There are many misconceptions here and it's something of a surprise that anybody ever manages to get the whole thing working in a way that is truly satisfactory. Sadly, most do not. Instead they settle for something which they believe is as good as they can get... but for most, things can be improved enormously. Here are a few common problems, though it's certainly not an exhaustive list (it leaves out things which might need professional help, such as erectile failure in the male and pain on penetration in the female):

- He is too fast.

- She does not get very aroused.
- He cannot sustain long enough.
- She wants it to go for too long.
- He always wants to look at her face.
- She hates being looked at.

Although we will investigate each of these situations separately, remedies are not discussed here, since this is not a book about improving your sex life but about understanding why things do not always work the way we want them to. There is plenty of sound advice available on the internet and an excellent site can be found at http://www.vitalogica.co.uk. This is an 'holistic' mind and body site with many problem areas explored in detail, some downloadable help files and an enormous amount of useful information.

Now we will look at those situations listed above:

He is too fast. This is a quite common problem and it's easy for a couple to believe that he is suffering from premature ejaculation. This, though, is not necessarily the case because there is quite a difference between that state and simply finishing before she is 'ready'. If it *is* premature ejaculation, then he knows all about it. Contrary to what his partner might believe, he has little, if any, satisfaction as a result since the ejaculatory sensation is extremely weak. Often, though, premature ejaculation is not truly the problem and something different is happening, again related to our ancient history. During intercourse, a male was extraordinarily vulnerable and so it was desirable to finish quickly in order to avoid the possibility of being eaten by a predator of some sort! So this tendency to speed is at least in part inherited and in this case the ejaculation will be completely satisfactory – for him. Whether it is true 'PE' or just that he is quick, professional help can do much to improve the situation and **Chapter Seventeen** – *Can therapy help?* will provide useful information.

She does not get very aroused. This is usually because he does not give her the time to. While a healthy male can be 'ready to go' in moments, a female needs much longer, within an established relationship. It's not just the mind but the physical body that works differently, and a fact that is something of a surprise to many is that she is capable of **seven times** the amount of sexual pleasure that the male can experience. She has the same number of pleasure sensors in the clitoris that the male has in the penis – but compressed into a much smaller area, intensifying the sensations. In addition to that, the pleasure centre in her brain is larger and far more active at the moment of orgasm than his is at the point of ejaculation. The male who learns patience and takes the trouble to discover a few techniques can greatly enhance his and her lovemaking experience.

He cannot sustain long enough. This is not the same thing as being too fast and is sometimes just that he gets past the point where he can continue. It might be that he runs out of energy or that his erection suddenly fails (which *might* be because of a medical condition). At other times, he just cannot hold on to the ejaculation for as long as his partner wants him to. He is actually not designed to last for very long and the answer is for him to wait until the female is *truly* ready and eager before getting inside her.

She wants it to go for too long. Most males have trouble understanding the 'plateau phase' of sex that a woman can experience – he just doesn't have one. For the male, once arousal has reached a peak there is an almost physically unstoppable urge to ejaculate. A female can reach a peak and stay there for ages, savouring the exquisite sensations in her entire body, finger tip to finger tip, head to toe. This is quite unlike the male response, which is localised to an area around the genitals, though there may be a salivation response just before ejaculation – the so-called 'vinegar stroke'. If he was able to achieve the plateau (as some older males can) he would also want to stay there for as long as possible! Again, the answer is to not start too early, allowing foreplay to arouse his partner to the plateau phase. It's fair to say, though, that she needs to be aware that once he has ejaculated, attempts to sustain intercourse will usually result in physical discomfort for him.

He always wants to look at her face. This is very much a 'male thing'. To him, his partner's face as she approaches orgasm is incredibly exciting and confirmation that she is truly enjoying what they are doing, which is genuinely important to him. If it *does* have something to do with male ego, as some people have claimed (*"Hey! Look how well I'm doing here!"*), he certainly is not aware of that. As far as he is concerned, watching her as she achieves orgasm is just the most astonishingly erotic experience, something that he might well fantasise about on occasions.

She hates being looked at. This is a common female response. The problem for many a woman is a deep belief that she somehow looks ugly as she approaches orgasm. She is aware of the involuntary tension in the muscles around the mouth and nose and it's difficult for her to imagine that her partner adores this! Probably for this reason, many females have a reflexive habit of turning their head to the side at the moment of orgasm and may even bury their face into the pillow as far as they are able to.

Masturbation

Masturbation is a fact of life. Most people do it, even when they are in a good relationship, although some people find the need to insist that they do not. An uncomfortable aspect of this particular activity is that if a female discovers her partner masturbating, she will not infrequently view it as infidelity and might well behave as if she has discovered him having sexual intercourse with another female. Males, however, are different. If a male discovers his partner masturbating, he will certainly not view it as infidelity, though he might become angry that she preferred to do that instead of have sex with him. More likely, though, is that he might become rapidly aroused and want to watch – or join in. The simple fact is that it's a different form of sex. For some people the climax is more intense – and, indeed, some females are not able to achieve orgasm by sexual intercourse, though can easily do so 'manually'. There is a difference in the way that males and females 'work' in this respect, in that a female will usually concentrate on the sensations in her body, where a male will usually be visualising a favoured fantasy. The important thing to recognise is that it's a healthy behaviour, both physically and emotionally, and *mutual* masturbation can be an enjoyable part of a couple's sex life.

The American comedian, Woody Allen, summed it up nicely when he said: *"Hey, don't knock masturbation – it's sex with someone you love!"*

Generalisations and exceptions

Although it's entirely possible to state how most people function sexually, there are always exceptions. Sometimes, they seem to deny the 'norm' while at other times they confirm it. Four commonly observed situations are covered here.

1   When young, the human male lives for sex, even though he will manage to suspend the urge under certain circumstances such as work or illness of a partner. Although social considerations will usually prevent him from following his deeper instincts, he is designed to pursue it relentlessly, scheme for it and even kill for it. Of course, all those behaviours are exhibited from time to time, though not by all males, fortunately. And yet, at the other extreme, he can be apparently completely disinterested in it when within the confines of an established relationship. He might even sometimes prefer watching football! This is usually evidence of boredom; it's a danger signal and needs

addressing sooner rather than later.

2   A female does not need to pursue sex because it will come to her. But sometimes, something unusual happens. She 'switches on' to a particular individual, occasionally even a totally unsuitable partner, and becomes more obsessive in her pursuit than any male might be. The female character in the film 'Fatal Attraction' is a dramatised but nonetheless reasonably accurate portrayal of this situation, illustrating clearly the determination not to be refused, and the extreme possessiveness, that is part of the associated behaviour pattern.

3   Some females seem not to have the 'buffer zone' mentioned earlier, instead thinking and behaving like a male, as far sexuality is concerned. They are sexual huntresses and there may even be a genetic inheritance at work. It's so natural to them that they might imagine that all females are the same. Males are usually wary of, and sometimes acutely uncomfortable with, such a female because they have not inherited the instinctive behaviour to be at ease with a sexually demanding individual. This is not to say that they don't like it; most do, up to a point. It's when they realise that they can't switch it off that they begin to have trouble coping and may even become distressed by it.

4   Some males never exhibit the sexual fascination that is usually quite evident and it's easy to assume that such an individual is a 'closet gay'. This is not necessarily the case, though. It's entirely possible that he is what is known as 'asexual', devoid of not only the 'permanently on' drive of the usual male, but of any interest whatsoever. Just occasionally, completely normal urges are present, though they are tightly controlled and severely inhibited by shyness, poor self-worth or masturbatory guilt. In these circumstances, a gentle sexual advance by a female will

unleash a sudden flood of obvious maleness!

It's worth being aware that any sexual behaviour that seems to be outside that which is considered 'normal' *can sometimes* be the result of a physical illness or a psychological condition. The symptoms, for that is what they are, can include (in no particular order): *Male disinterest; female extra interest; exhibitionism; excessive shyness; male failure to ejaculate; female failure to orgasm; anger at sexual advances; inability to sustain arousal; anxiety at arousal; pain on penetration; anxiety on penetration; after-sex nausea; sexual obsession/addiction.*

Most of those conditions can be caused by either physical or psychological processes and all can be helped more often than not. A later chapter describes various different resources and where to find them.

The role of personality in sex

An individual's personality type definitely has some bearing on the way that they function in a sexual relationship. People may vary greatly, though, and the following is offered as an aid to understanding, rather than a definitive guide to how any particular person might behave. It can help you to recognise if what happens in *your* love life would be considered to be within the bounds of 'normal'.

The Warrior: The Warrior personality is control-based and therefore is usually not particularly demonstrative. Romantic and emotional responses are rather thin on the ground and this individual can become noticeably uncomfortable if such behaviour is suggested or given in excess. Direct and to the point, the Warrior dislikes refusals or demands. Quick to criticise, they cannot easily stand criticism being levelled at them and will seek to turn the tables. A sexual relationship with another Warrior is likely to be extremely stormy and neither person will find it easy to talk about their wishes and dislikes.

Male Warriors really want their partner to always say 'yes' whether she wants to or not. A 'no' response feels like rejection and they will either argue or sulk – or both, in that order. They will not easily change their attitude but might eventually do so with a strong partner, though this can occasionally result in some kind of sexual difficulty. If that should happen, they will find a way to make sure that their partner realises that is *their* fault.

Female Warriors often try to limit the amount of sexual activity to no more than they want themselves. Insistence from the male can produce a sharp rebuke and/or a warning of cessation of activity altogether for a while. This attitude will only change unwillingly and will often result in a symptom designed to make sex impossible for the partner. Vaginismus is a good example; thrush is another, though neither is voluntary, of course.

The Settler: The Settler is concerned with feelings and emotions at least as much as with the physical sensations involved with sexuality. Most of the time, sex, especially sexual intercourse, is only properly satisfactory if the emotional state is right; frantic sex in the middle of an argument is definitely not for this one. The inherited need for security often leads to an anxiety that they are not pleasing their partner but they find it difficult to ask, for fear of ridicule, disgust or rejection. A relationship with another Settler can be difficult, since both can sometimes hesitate to take the lead in case the other is 'not in the mood'. This means that they may wait for some sign from their partner – who is anxious about giving it for fear of rejection.

Male Settlers are usually considerate and mindful of their partner's emotional needs and well-being. They will be quietly romantic though are not always good at demonstrating passion. Complicated in his responses, if he experiences rejection often enough, he will soon begin to feel as if it's *him*, rather than sex that is being rejected. This response is actually quite common to most males but is often the source of psychosexual difficulty for the male Settler.

Female Settlers are kind and caring to their partner as a rule and will 'do' sex even when they are not 'in the mood', just because they can... as long as they love their partner. If they stop loving and/or trusting him, then they will often become very stubborn, or perhaps passively and silently compliant, since sexual activity then feels wrong. Under those circumstances, it's not unusual for them to completely lose interest and they will be unlikely to 'thaw' unless they manage to re-establish trust and feelings of love. Fortunately, perhaps, that's more likely with this personality than any other.

The Nomad: The Nomad personality usually has a strong and highly passionate sex drive and a low level of inhibition. They like to experiment and can sometimes have a problem with faith-fulness, mainly because of a low boredom threshold and a ready eye for the opposite sex. They are concerned with both their own image and that of their partner – they want their partner to think *they* are sexy and want their partner to look sexy as well. They can be romantic and outrageously flirty. A relationship with another Nomad can be excellent as far as sex is concerned, since they will both be seeking to achieve the maximum enjoyment, though there can often be a 'what about me?' response if anything goes wrong.

Male Nomads are usually more personable than the other two types but have a tendency towards self-centeredness and can sometimes be quite shallow. This can lead to anger and frustration if anything – even a partner's illness – gets in the way of their own gratification. They can suffer prolonged sexual diffi-culty if their partner is dismissive so it's not a surprise that that's when they are most likely to stray.

Female Nomads are often very sexy to look at but may not actually 'perform' as well as their appearance suggests they will. It's also possible that their level of interest in sex is lower than they appear to be signalling. This is possibly because a lot of their sexual energy is being discharged in their presentation of self. When they *are* interested, they are often very passionate, active and noisy and will have no difficulties in initiating sex. If they should develop uncertainty about their physical attractiveness though, they may lose interest in sex altogether.

And finally...

This chapter has been all about problems and misunderstandings that can occur as a result of the major differences between males and females as far as sex and sexual behaviour is concerned. It's completely fair to say that most females will find the male attitude annoying, selfish, childish, and even obnoxious some of the time. It's equally fair to say that most males will occasionally find the female attitude bafflingly incomprehensible, aggravating and frustrating. The fact is, though, that both are only doing what they know how to do and are responding to inherited instincts, rather than seeking to punish, hurt, or manipulate each other. Understanding this fairly simple fact can lead to far greater harmony in the bedroom which can spread into the rest of life.

Sex and sexuality is a huge subject that could easily make at least three books all on its own but we have looked at enough here to help you in your current or future relationships. To be on the safe side, though, there is more about it in the next chapter...

You might be in for something of a surprise...

Chapter Six

Sex, sexuality, secrets and lies

Sex can be passionate, loving, sweaty, romantic, animalistic, exhausting, inspiring, exhilarating, quick, slow, unwilling, joyful, hard work, spontaneous, experimental, awkward, embarrassing, ecstatically crude, wonderfully rude and much more besides. No wonder it's the cause of so many problems and difficulties! In the last chapter we looked at problems and misunderstandings that can arise out of the differences in the way that men and women 'work' sexually. In this one, we look at a few of the common issues that can affect relationships generally, and sex and sexuality in particular.

Not always joyful...

It is a fact that there will be times for everybody, no matter how good the relationship is, when sex just doesn't work very well. Sometimes, it can be put down to just the random events of life – the telephone rings in the middle of it, the dog jumps on the bed, somebody knocks at the door, or even a sudden attack of hiccups. But those things can – and should – be recognised and accepted for what they actually are. Irritating but just a one-off that won't spoil the next time. (Although to be on the safe side, it's probably a good idea to keep animals out of the bedroom... Most men *hate* being stared at by the dog while they're in the middle of it!)

All those things and others like them are unavoidable and nobody's 'fault'. Often, though, difficulties arise almost by stealth. Totally avoidable issues sneak up on us over a period of time until they're entrenched in the 'fabric' of the relationship and extraordinarily difficult to change. Not impossible though, as long as both halves of the couple are able to see the problem and can agree on an attempt to resolve it without criticism or reproach. They will need to tackle it honestly without either of them making claims along the lines of: *"See? I've always said that!"* and also with a willingness to let go of past hurts and irritations. In other words, they have to truly *want* to make things better. For both of them. Later in this book, there is some advice to help you create that exact situation.

And if it proves too late to rescue the relationship you're in, or if you're not in one right now, what you learn here will help you to make the next one better!

Antisexual behaviour

This has to be at the top of the list of avoidable issues and though it can take many forms, they all have one thing in common... they're a complete 'turn off' for most people! Males and females are equally guilty, though they might not realise it – or if they do, they might consider it to be unimportant. It's almost always something you just would not do in front of your partner in the early stages of a relationship, yet scarcely notice as familiarity increases and inhibition fades. Digging around in your nose with your fingernail is a good example – especially if you visually inspect whatever you find there afterwards before doing whatever you do with it. Breaking wind noisily and fanning the air with your hand while pulling a face is another. You get the idea, and there are many other simply 'unsexy' behaviours. Of course, you might now be thinking stuff like that is not such a big deal in a familiar relationship and might even be humorous... But how does it feel if your partner has been doing that during the evening and then enquires whether you 'fancy an early night'? Unless you have a fetish for that sort of thing, it's unlikely to be a good line in seduction.

Over a period of time, such things gradually 'chip away' at personal attractiveness... and if you lose enough of *that*, sexiness goes out the window. The biggest problem here is that it all becomes part of the overall balance between 'sexy' and 'unsexy'. The more the balance leans towards 'sexy', the better the relationship will be as far as sexuality is concerned. There's more about this later in the chapter but first, we're going to have a look at something that far too often gets in the way of sorting out problems.

Talk resistance

It's well enough known that when a relationship hits problems, whether those problems are about sex or something else entirely, it's almost impossible to sort things out without talking about what's wrong. But defensiveness, recrimination and total misunderstanding can cause more difficulty than the original problem did in the first place. And yet, paying attention to a couple of quite basic rules can make life a lot easier all round – and we're not talking here about dealing with full-blown arguments (we do that later in the book) but about how to address an issue, perhaps one of those antisexual behaviours, without it escalating into a major row. It has as much to do with tone of voice as it does the actual words that are said, and it's the 'opening line' that can generate resistance to the rest of the conversation.

"We need to talk."

This is one of the worst ways to begin, even though it might well be the most commonly used. Because the phrase is so well known, being used in films and stories and almost always associated with problems, most people have an instantly negative response towards it. Not only that, it's often delivered in an almost confrontational manner and definitely tips the balance heavily towards 'unsexy'. Pretty much the same can be said for: *"I want a word with you,"* usually delivered with a slightly aggrieved tone. The response to either 'opener' depends on the personality of the listener but it's unlikely to be positive:

- The **Warrior** will prepare for battle and be likely to say something like: *"Oh, good, here we go again!"*

- The **Settler** will become anxious and might respond with: *"Oh no... What've I done now?'*
- The **Nomad** will become belligerent: *"Oh, I haven't got time for all that stuff right now!"*

After that, there's little or no chance that anything positive will be gained from the conversation – and there may not even be one. The Warrior will be expecting to cover old ground, and will be certain to do so; the Settler will be expecting some sort of admonishment and will feel it, even if it's not meant; and the Nomad will attempt to escape by walking away from the whole thing. The most likely outcome is that there's no change. Back to the 'same old, same old'.

But it doesn't have to be that way... What if, instead of: *"We need to talk,"* something less doom-laden had been used instead. Something neutral like: *"Have you got a minute?"* Asked at a sensible time, most people are going to give a 'yes' response and they are now already involved with the conversation instead of being defensively on the outside of it. What comes after that is important, of course.

- **Good**: *"Okay... Look, I really want our sex life to improve, and..."*
- **Not good**: *"You put me right off sex when you..."*

In other words, resisting the temptation for criticism, recrimination or telling a few 'home truths', is far more likely to resolve the issue. 'I' statements are always better and less confrontational than 'You' statements and if you care about the relationship, this is important. It's as well to be aware that if you actually *want* a confrontation (the 'finally having it out' situation) and that's not unknown, then there are almost certainly deeper problems than whatever you are seeking to resolve. There's help in a later chapter for that situation.

Now, what about an antidote if that 'we need to talk' is addressed to you? No matter what your personality group, you can defuse the situation easily: *"Okay – but have you got a minute first?"* You are now 'carrying the ball' and you can continue with: *"Only, I've been feeling as if you're not happy, so let's see if we can sort out whatever's wrong."* If disarming your partner is possible, you've now done exactly that – and if it's *not* possible, then the relationship may be in more trouble than it seemed... but, again, there's help for that later.

Little secrets

Some people claim that a relationship cannot survive unless it's based on openness, honesty and truth and that there's no time or place for secrets or lies. That is a nice, though somewhat lofty, ideal – but it's not necessarily true. The truth is that some relationships will survive joyously and harmoniously precisely *because of* secrets, as long as they are kept. Little ones, that is. (Your subconscious can make the big ones lethal, as you will soon see). If it *is* just a *little* secret and you're keeping it because you genuinely don't want to cause some sort of hurt to another, then it's a *good thing* and your subconscious will be at ease with it.

For instance, it might be the case that one of your previous relationships is not exactly a secret, but the fact that you were absolutely besotted, more than with anybody before or since, is. Well, letting your current partner know that they're second best isn't going to enhance your relationship, is it? That's a good secret to keep and there's no need for damaging guilt. Maybe you fantasise about a film star or somebody else during masturbation. *That* is definitely a good secret to keep! Likewise if you find something sexually stimulating that you know your partner might find peculiar or even revolting (it does happen) in which case you should keep it quiet and save it for those deeply intense and private solo moments. And if you secretly lust after your partner's best friend...

Big secrets

So what about the big ones?

A lot depends on the reason you might keep them. If it's because of guilt or fear, then it will haunt you and your subconscious will almost certainly see to it that you let the cat out of the bag at some point. This is the way we're designed and there's no escape. We all know that thing where it's important in some situation or other that you don't talk about a particular subject or concept, and yet it keeps on popping into your mind... and often out of your mouth in an unguarded instant. It's one of those *"What on earth did I have to go and say that for?"* moments that most of us have experienced.

The reason is simple enough. If there's something in the mind that's a potential threat (and guilt or fear are associated with threat) then the subconscious insists that it's active in everything we do so we can be on our guard against it. Unfortunately, that subconscious gets things a bit mixed up on occasions and leads to us wanting to *talk* about whatever's on our mind, even though that can cause big problems. We've all felt it, that urge to 'spit out' whatever is bothering us, even when we consciously know it's not really a good idea. So if your secret is a *BIG* one based on guilt or fear, you're probably going to have to work hard to keep it safe. And it should go without saying that the bigger it is the harder will be the work needed to keep it.

Now we're going to get into some rather 'dark' territory and though you might wrinkle your nose at some of it, it's all about helping to keep sex alive and joyful and your relationships healthy. For some people, that can occasionally mean behaving in a way that others might not understand... So it's a good thing that they don't have to know about it!

We'll dive into these most murky of waters straight away – but do, just for a few moments, suspend moral judgement and any self-righteous snorting! We're talking here about the situation where somebody who is already in a loving relationship indulges for whatever reason in a 'one-night-stand'. Not an ongoing affair, just a one-off event about which, immediately the heat of passion has faded, they feel sick with guilt about and are resolved beyond doubt that it will never, ever, happen again. You can put forward all sorts of arguments about morals, about not wanting to do it with anybody else if the relationship is good, about how if they truly loved their partner, and so on. But the fact remains that for the human animal, once the sex-drive switch in the brain goes fully into the 'on' position, the responsibility switch goes 'off'.

*We're **not** saying here that it's forgivable, that it's okay or understandable or putting forward any other mitigating circumstance. We're saying that it happens. It happens to men and women who never intended it to but whose moral code got hi-jacked for a few fleeting seconds by nature. And when it comes to a battle between morals and nature, nature will usually find a way to win.*

So now what? There are really only two options:

- *Tell their partner in an attempt to get rid of some of the guilt.* This might make them feel better (though it might not) but will cause pain for their partner, and what has been a loving relationship is now over. 'Serves them right' you might say... But now their partner is suffering too, even though they don't deserve to.
- *Keep it secret and carry the guilt for as long as it takes.* As long as the erring individual is truly seeking to avoid causing monstrous hurt to their partner, that old saying: 'what the eye doesn't see, the heart doesn't grieve over' is very relevant here. Loving and nurturing can continue and if the 'protecting partner instinct' is stronger than the urge for the preservation of integrity of self, then there's a good

chance the secret will be kept. Though there is a price...

Many people will want to insist that the second option is immoral, dishonest, disloyal, deceitful, under-handed... and it might be all those things. That's the price, the burden that has to be carried. There are all sorts of reproachful 'what ifs' that can be levelled, too. BUT the best 'what if' is: 'What if that relationship continues to be joyous and loving and the partner never finds out about that one moment of infidelity?' At least there's a chance that two people will remain happy rather than suffering the sort of devastation from which it's never easy to recover.

Sometimes, a secret really does need to be kept.

No matter what it is, it should remain a secret forever, not just be stored up to be blurted out in an argument at some point. Not shared with your friends to relieve the guilt, however close they might be. And what others would think if they knew about it doesn't come into it, nor does what you believe others might do. It's your life and your relationship, your choice. And it's your secret.

Little lies, big lies

It's an interesting thing that the way anybody thinks about lying, and therefore what they will deem acceptable, depends to a large extent on their personality type:

- **Warrior** individuals will insist that a lie is a lie and have no truck with 'little white lies' at all (unless they're telling them.) They demand the *whole* truth and are good at winkling it out once they start. So if your partner is a Warrior, it's probably best to lie only when you really need to and then stick to your guns with a straight face, no matter what. Just as they do – they're past masters of the 'honest glare'.
- **Settler** people will know that a white lie designed to look

after somebody's feelings is perfectly acceptable. They usually know when somebody is lying though may choose to just let it go. They can easily feel hurt because of it, though, so if your partner is a Settler, be kind! They are not generally very good at lying themselves.

- **Nomads** are usually not the quickest at spotting a lie. When they do, though, they tend to tell everybody they know with not a shred of embarrassment. If your partner is a Nomad and you must lie, be sure to incorporate it into some sort of praise for them and you'll probably get away with it. Excellent story-tellers, there are few who can lie as well as this group!

Now, all of the above really refer to 'little white lies'. It is impossible to sustain a relationship without a few of those being bandied around from time to time. Many orgasms are fake; a gift might *not* be wonderful; your body might *not* be just as sexy as it ever was; the late office meeting might have been in the pub; the fraught day might have been spent shopping; *"This? I've had it for ages!"* might mean *"I bought it yesterday'."* And all that's without the likes of: 'I've got a bit of a headache, actually...'

The point is, little lies like those are part and parcel of a relationship and you shouldn't lose too much sleep over them. They don't mean your relationship is on the rocks or that love is fading, whether you are telling them or hearing them. Quite the reverse, in fact, since they are an indication that you still care what each other thinks. You are still important to each other. These little fibs don't require an elaborate 'back story' that has to be remembered, and they are not disguising anything that would cause great pain if the truth came out, most of the time.

Big lies, though, are a different animal altogether. Having an illicit affair, running up gambling debts, involvement in anything illegal, losing your employment, stealing from your partner... all these situations are potentially catastrophically damaging. If you find yourself involved with anything similar *and* you want to save your relationship, they must be addressed as soon as possible. Your efforts might be in vain but at least then you're free to pursue a new future earlier than if you just wait for the inevitable. For that's what it is. A big lie almost always becomes steadily more elaborate each time it has to be told and it's only a matter of time before there is an obvious contradiction in the story.

Sexy is as sexy does...

Well, that was all getting a bit heavy there, so let's lighten things up a bit by getting back to being sexy. If you still want to be seen as sexy to your partner, then you need to be sexy *for* your partner. It's all too easy to think it's a given and because you still do it, that sexuality in your relationship will stay alive and well without you having to do anything about it, but that's exactly how antisexual behaviour starts to creep in.

It's the brain that's the problem. In the beginning of the relationship, your natural body scent or the sound of your voice might well have acted as a stimulus for unbridled passion. But the brain is a peculiar bit of kit, getting used to those triggers until they do very little. In fact, if there has been enough unsexy stuff going on, they might have exactly the opposite effect. This is why, after you've been with somebody for a couple of years or so, you might have difficulty seeing them in the same way that others do – you're used to them and others are not. That's a dangerous situation by the way, because others will be more likely to see what you've lost sight of and find it attractive.

So you need to keep it all alive.

It's not difficult and we'll have a look at a few things that can move that balance towards 'sexy' and a few others that might well have the opposite effect.

Sexy: Be sure to tell your partner from time to time they are the sexiest thing on two legs. If you do that from the beginning it's easy; if it's been a while then you're probably subject to the 'bus stop syndrome', which makes it difficult, and you'll find out how to deal with that later in the book (in **Chapter Ten** – *Making a poor thing better*).

Unsexy: Commenting about spots, lines, saggy bits and wrinkles. We all know we're getting older and are soon enough confronted with the evidence in the mirror. But to believe that we are still found sexy goes a long way to offsetting the horror of it all!

Sexy: Flirting with your partner over a romantic meal and wine, either at home or a luxury restaurant or hotel. Eye contact is magnetic, a touch of the hand can be electric, and murmured words of endearment even more so.

Unsexy: Males – making it obvious you're *expecting* sex and/or getting angry when it doesn't happen for whatever reason. Females – changing your mind for no good reason after you've been giving signals all evening.

Sexy: Respecting sexual arousal even when you're not aroused. If your partner is horny but you really *cannot* do intercourse for whatever reason, then rubbing, licking, stroking and massaging until they climax is almost as good.

Unsexy: Dismissing your partner's sexual arousal by saying things like: *"Sorry – not in the mood."*; *"Haven't got time for all that..."* or worst of all: *"For god's sake put it away will you?"*

Sexy: Sounding interested when your partner wants to tell you about something, even if you don't really know what they're talking about.

Unsexy: Sounding bored when your partner wants to tell you about something that clearly interests them.

There are obviously a lot more of those 'rules' but you get the idea and if you analyse them you'll discover they all come down to the same thing – respect for your partner. Now, if you grew up in a house where there was little or no respect, you might need to have a long think about who would be happiest – somebody who followed the above ideas, or somebody who behaved as those you grew up with did? Perhaps what you experienced in your younger years has taught you it's a totally natural thing to be constantly resisting what your partner wants to do, always trying to find some way of staying in control, maybe even scoring 'points' whenever you can. You can think of that as 'auto-contrariness', choosing to always disagree with your partner. Again, though, how does that help you to be happy with this person for the rest of your life? And how is it making your partner happy? Of course, you might believe that all this 'happiness in relationships' nonsense doesn't truly exist, that it's a kind of propaganda put about by those who are a bit 'soft'... But supposing you're wrong? Wouldn't you want some of what so many others actually do have?

The balance

We'll finish this chapter with a quick look at the way the brain works – you'll soon see why this is so important. It actually never forgets any sort of pattern once it's been encountered, which is why you can sometimes take an instant like or dislike to somebody the instant you meet them. In just a split second, your brain analyses everything it can about them and compares what it finds with everyone else you already know – or have ever known. If there is a reasonable match for *like* or *dislike*, it fires up that same response. You don't have any choice in the matter. You feel whatever you feel without even stopping to work out why. And even if somebody assures you that an individual you've met is a wonderful person, when you really aren't so keen, you'll harbour doubts for ages, until you've seen enough 'evidence' to convince you to change your mind.

So why is this so important in relationships? Well, it's that 'sexy/unsexy' balance. You see, that brain of yours is constantly evaluating everything for every spilt second of everyday, making tiny changes where there's enough energy to demand it, and that energy is created by our emotional responses. Maybe you're beginning to 'get it' already, but just in case:

From the very beginning of the relationship, every 'sexy' event creates a favourable emotional response and every 'unsexy' event creates an unfavourable response. When the balance is towards 'favourable' the relationship is working nicely but when it is more towards 'unfavourable', work is needed to get back on track.

Okay, so that's a very 'rough and ready' example of the way the brain works, because some things will create a much stronger emotional response than others, so there's that to take into account too. Having sex with somebody else might tip the balance completely, of course, while saying: *"Not tonight, darling,"* might cause only a mere quiver... but you get the idea. Relationships need looking after, and from the very start.

You might now be thinking, quite rightly, that relationships are about more than sex and sexuality, however fundamental to happiness that might be. And that's what we're going to be looking at in the rest of the book.

Chapter Seven

The three men that women want

*It's important to recognise that the first part of this chapter is not intended as an accurate portrayal of the lives of our ancient ancestors, but as a story to illustrate the biological processes of the human animal. It's a chapter for the ladies, but men might discover what those ladies **really** want!*

It's tough for women to find the sort of man they want these days. That's not because men are somehow becoming less attractive or desirable (though a good few women might argue about that!) but because of a conflict between biology and intellect.

It was different thousands of years ago. Although they might not have had a great deal of say in who they coupled with, it was easy to decide which male they actually wanted. It would the one who was skilled enough as a hunter to bring home the biggest hunk of wild boar, who would probably also be the one most likely to be able to protect them when the going got tough. So, a big guy, scared of little and certainly stuffed full of resource that was unmistakably *male.*

But maybe not. Maybe it was totally different. Perhaps, in those days, they didn't even think about trying to find all those attributes in just *one* male... After all, there were probably not the social restrictions we have in place today. The truth is nobody really knows exactly what their social and relationship arrangements were, or even if they had any. Perhaps they wanted to bag a Hunter to 'bring home the bacon', a Protector to keep them safe, and a Lover to... Well, you get the picture. The 'bait' was sex and so it was that the female who seemed to be the most enticing would get the pick of the males. And of course, the males who were best at their particular skill would get the pick of the females, so it's easy to imagine that competition between the males would have been pretty intense. And this is where the whole idea falls down... It falls down because, just as in the animal world today, the males will compete against each other until only one has 'breeding rights' with any particular female. So the Hunter, the Protector and the Lover, each 'winners' in their own right, would all compete in a kind of 'final', the victor taking the prize and the female getting the overall best of the three.

She might not have got the whole three males she originally wanted but whichever one she ended up with, it's a fair bet that he was big, successful, and could provide security and father her children. (One or some of them, anyway, because monogamy and pair-bonding has never been part of the 'human condition'.) In fact, the one thing that all three had in common was that they were *big*, otherwise they could not have fought off the others.

Yes, of course it's all a bit of a flight of fancy, since we have no way of knowing exactly how life was back then. But now let's cycle forward a few thousand years to the present. One thing in particular has changed quite drastically and as you will soon see, it's that change that causes problems.

All in the genes

Evolution moves very slowly so the descendants of those ancient people still 'work' in the same way as their ancestors, and it's still the most enticing female who gets the pick of the males. But there's a problem. The most successful modern Hunter male doesn't do it in the forest with a spear or a net, but in the world of business. He doesn't use his body but his brain, and it's his salary that's evidence of his prowess, not the size of the 'kill' that he brings home. So now one of the genetic 'markers' of the successful male is badly skewed. Although this is a bit of a sweeping generalisation, it carries a lot of truth:

- The most financially successful male is usually not built like his ancient ancestors.
- The male who is built like his ancestors is usually not the most financially successful.

There are exceptions of course, in the males who are built like 'real men' who also manage to earn a high wage, but there are far fewer of those than their slimmer and less physical counterparts. So the modern female now has to wrestle with a conflict that just didn't exist for her forbears. The big and sexy male – the potential Lover (who might also double as the Protector) – might not provide the security of the slimmer, financially successful but less overtly sexy one – the Hunter (who might also double as the Protector.) The conflict is between the instinctive urge for sex and the desire for security, and unless it's addressed, it's a recipe for disappointment!

It is this very conflict that might be the cause of that well-known marriage-wrecking situation, the pursuit of a 'bit of rough'. And it might also be the reason the fantasy figures portrayed by male strippers are so often based on a major signal of authority... the uniform. It's easy to see a Policeman or Fireman as a 'real man'.

It's actually not all that unusual for a woman to insist that she's not really interested in muscular males. Well, maybe she's more evolved than those who throw their knickers on the stage at a male strip show. Maybe she's already resolved the conflict between muscular sexiness and intelligent security. But it's entirely possible she's simply denying the urges of her subconscious! Of course, this is not to say that a female won't find a slim man sexy – many do, and form splendid and long-lasting relationships with them. But usually, they have *discovered* he's sexy rather than knowing it the moment they laid eyes on him.

There's something else to take into account as well – it was probably quite normal for our ancestors not to have a regular partner at all but a succession of sexual couplings with different individuals. So the male who won the 'breeding rights' with a particular female would probably have been looking at some other female before long. The relationship was never intended to be anything other than fleeting. These days, though, most people (not all!) eventually want more than that, which leads us into something of enormous importance: the best match for a long-term relationship never *was* built on sexuality on its own. No matter how enticing that sexual draw is, however much it rocks your boat, it will almost certainly fade sooner rather than later. And then you're left with the underlying Hunter, Protector or Lover sharing your life, your home and your bed. You need to feel emotionally connected and we don't really have any idea how much of that is associated with instinct. It might even be an entirely modern phenomenon, something that we hang on to as a 'crutch' to help us survive with just one partner.

The answer

Fortunately, there's a way for a female to at least have a good idea what she's getting herself into right from the start and it's easier than you might think! It's all about the combination of your own personality and that of a potential partner. You can do it by having another look at **Chapter Three** – *The way people are and the games they play* – where you see how a relationship with each type would work for you, or you can take the slightly more specific approach shown here. We've been referring so far throughout this chapter to the Hunter, Protector and Lover, and they correspond to Warrior, Settler and Nomad but are concerned solely with their sexuality:

- The **Warrior** is the Hunter – observant, quick to see how to 'catch someone out', and able to manipulate their prey to their advantage. Emotions are reigned in and they will not often tell you they love you, fearing that it weakens them in some way. Sexually controlled, they need encouragement to become demonstrative and might be distant or non-committal immediately afterwards.

- The **Settler** is the Protector – though not necessarily in a physical manner. They will usually put you before themselves and will find a way to deal with most life problems and make it look easy. They are often tougher than they seem but tend to 'wear their heart on their sleeve' and have no trouble telling you they love you. Sexually under-confident sometimes, they might need reassurance in their ability to satisfy you.

- The **Nomad** is the Lover – usually with a Capital 'L'! Expressive and charismatic, they can be impressive when it comes to illustrating how much they care for you, but some of it might be mainly for show. Usually sexually adventurous, they like to experiment and might get bored easily, when they will tend to rely on you to find something exciting to spice it up. There can be a problem with fickleness.

It is entirely possible, even probable, that your man will be a combination of two of the types, in which case you can seek to strengthen the part you like best! Or just enjoy both, of course... Usually, though, you will discover over a period of time that one of those traits is the one most commonly active.

Now, female Warriors, Settlers and Nomads don't work in the same way and don't group into the same categories. Instead, we have:

- The **Warrior** is the Goddess – the one who seeks to control pretty much everything in her environment, including her man, and usually manages it well. More often than not a no-nonsense individual, she demands equality with her partner. Sexually, she may not be over-demonstrative, though as a rule has no trouble achieving orgasm, which she might 'do' fairly quietly.

- The **Settler** is the Earth Mother – taking care of those around her and making sure their needs are met as far as possible. She will put her man's well-being ahead of her own and will fiercely defend him against the criticism of others, since she is a 'tough cookie' underneath the soft exterior. Sexually undemanding, she will usually be happy to do it when her man wants to, though might be reluctant to take the lead.

- The **Nomad** is the Courtesan or Harlot – and she can choose which, slotting into elegant or 'slutty' roles as she feels like it and as her man desires. She will usually be noisily demonstrative in sex, seeking – and often finding – huge or multiple orgasms. She does not usually find domesticity a very attractive proposition but will cope with it as long as there is excitement in the offing *somewhere* in her life.

From the above, you might already be able to work out good pairings... But it is also entirely possible to make a relationship that's *not* ideal work perfectly well as long as you take certain elements into account. This is a good thing indeed, for if the power of *chemistry* calls you, then you can be sure to do all that you need to keep that particular bit of magic alive and well! We'll have a look at a few possibilities, their snags and how you might cope.

The Goddess and the Hunter

This is potentially the 'worst' relationship of all! It would be two Warriors together and you might remember the advice in **Chapter Three** that this is unlikely to be a relationship that will last... but recognition of a like-minded soul might draw you into it, aided and abetted by chemistry. If that's the case, then to get the best out of it, it's important that you both find agreement about your roles in the relationship. As long as you can both work out where each of you are allowed to be in control in your life together; as long as you can accept that just because he doesn't say it doesn't mean he doesn't love you; and as long as you both agree firmly that any dissent will be talked about in a *controlled* and respectful manner (taking into account some of the other advice in this book), it can work. The Warrior is usually more practical than the other two groups and that gives you – literally – a fighting chance of success. There are probably better relationships for you... but if this is the one you want, and he wants you, then it's worth working at it to make it as harmonious as possible.

The Goddess and the Protector

This can actually work extremely well as long as you don't expect too much dynamism and ability to take charge of tricky situations, because he's likely to leave those to you to sort those out. But when it comes to understanding your hurts and disappointments, and finding constructive answers for them, there are few who do it this well. The major attribute he will show is patience – no matter how much of a 'strop' you throw (and, of course, this is something you do very well on occasions!) he will still love you and want to make things better. You should not, though, confuse this with weakness, because this person is generally not a 'quitter' and will continue to seek answers long after you might have decided there aren't any. He'll usually find them, too. There can be minor difficulties in your sex life together when he is trying to be gentle and loving and you really want him to just get on and **do it** – the best thing then, rather than say anything, is just to take charge of the situation... which he will like. This is not a showy person, nor a controlling one, but somebody who will seek to get the best out of your life together.

The Goddess and the Lover

This is potentially the best relationship for you, as long as you can handle the energy. The biggest problem you might encounter is a tendency to 'flakiness' and unreliability, though as long as you make it clear that you really don't tolerate such behaviour it will be greatly minimised. Sex is very important to this man and it's likely that you will find yourself doing it when you don't really want to, just to keep him quiet. If you love him, this won't concern you too much and it's important to recognise that his sexual urgency is usually greater than that of the Hunter or the Protector. This means that he might not be able to last as long as you really want to but it *will* be exciting and intense, as well as frequent. Image – yours and his – is important to him so he will always want both of you to look good when in the company of others and as a result your girlfriends are likely to envy you. He is likely to know this and may pander to it. The combination of his personality and your practicality can make you into a formidable couple.

The Earth Mother and the Hunter

This can be an excellent relationship as long as you don't expect the same amount of emotional warmth or effort back as you put into it. It doesn't mean he doesn't love you – he might just not want to say so. And there lies a possible conflict, for you are likely to be communicative and this man will not be – after all, he's descended from hunters, who didn't have time for a lot of chatter while chasing after the tribe's dinner! Your adaptability and willingness to accept the ways of others will usually allow you to be at ease with this though, and it's almost a 'given' that you will know beyond doubt you are looked after and safe. But this is a man who needs to be in control of every part of his life; it is entirely possible that he will expect you to do his bidding most of the time, including sexually, and can be quite 'put out' if refused. As long as you don't pander to this, and allow him to have his silent moods without comment from you, he'll get over it. If there's dissent at any time – which is almost inevitable – switching into your 'nurturing' mode will usually sort things out.

The Earth Mother and the Protector

This sort of relationship is potentially weak since although you will both seek to look after each other, neither one of you has that vital 'spark' to tackle the problems of life head on, preferring to let others do that. This means that when you hit some of the 'cosmic jokes' that the Universe dumps on us all from time to time, such things as sudden illness, money problems, aggressive neighbours and so on, you might not feel the reassurance that you would like to. Yes, he will care very much for you, but if what somebody else is doing is distressing you, he will seek to help you adapt to the situation, rather than find a way to resolve the issue. There will be few arguments, which is a good thing, but little in the way of excitement, so that life can become a bit 'humdrum', though it might be the case that you would be content with that. Sex is not going to be an exciting affair – quite the opposite, in fact, for he's likely to spend time wondering if you want to do it rather than making an exploratory move to find out. If you are at ease taking the initiative sometimes, that's not a problem. It's fair to say, though, that you are unlikely to bring out the best in each other.

The Earth Mother and the Lover

How this works depends very much on how you automatically respond to dynamically energetic individuals. If they inspire you and bring out your sense of fun, then this will be a wonderful union, albeit one that might worry you on occasions because of the apparent lack of concern about responsibilities. On the other hand, if charismatic individuals seem to you to be somewhat childish and noisy, then the best advice is to stay away from this one, no matter how hot he makes you and no matter how exciting the flirting and subsequent sex might be. Without an opposing energy to rein him in – which you might not have – this man can be embarrassingly outspoken, apparently bad mannered and *tiresome*. He is likely to see a relationship as revolving around him and his needs, unless he's with a partner who firmly reminds him from time to time that this is not necessarily the case. Having said that, life will never be dull and the sex will be frequent and expressive. If you think you can cope with all that, and actually enjoy it, this one's a 'keeper'.

The Courtesan and the Hunter

This *can* be a 'match made in Heaven'! The Hunter and the Courtesan are almost always drawn towards each other – she to the apparent strength and ability to maintain control, he to the decorous and sexy femininity that's being used to snare him (though he doesn't know that, of course!) The major problem that can arise here is in 'misleading advertising'; if you have given him the impression that you are in awe of his masculinity and are always ready to reward him with sex, then that's the way you have to remain with this one. If this is not the real you, he will be quick to notice that and will soon start to exert his controlling nature over you... before he walks away. As long as you are *genuinely* impressed by his strengths and enjoy being able to persuade or manipulate this control-orientated individual into believing that you are the most desirable female on the face of the earth, then this can be a great union. There is one thing to be aware of though, and that is that you will never *truly* know this man, any more than he will ever *truly* know you. But you will each *think* you know the other – and that can work like magic.

The Courtesan and the Protector

This can work, though it's possible that you will make the mistake of thinking that this man is weak... he isn't, but nor is he colourful or overtly 'macho'. What he is, is somebody with a deep sense of responsibility who will want to care for you and encourage you to get the best out of your life. He might also wonder, a lot of the time, why you have chosen to be with *him* and he'll need reassurance that you love his sensible way of being, and the way he cares for you more than anybody else has ever done (well, if you tell him that, he'll want to believe it and it will quietly delight him). He can provide a wonderful stabilising influence to your playful and sometimes slightly irresponsible nature which he is likely to adore, though he might occasionally seek to calm you down a little and it would be a good idea to go along with it if he does. Sexually, there is unlikely to be much in the way of swinging from the chandeliers, but what it lacks in adventure and experiment, it gains in depth of emotion and genuine love. You should allow yourself to enjoy that!

The Courtesan and the Lover

Potentially the worst possible of all relationships for you, this one could be a disaster! Tempestuous, sexual, noisy, aggravating, selfish and manipulative doesn't really get close to the possibilities associated with this pairing. The problem is that you would both be seeking the same thing – to be the centre of attention wherever you are and never wanting to praise the other since you're not getting praise yourself. You both have wonderful qualities but put the two of you together and they cancel each other out completely, resulting in a 'toxic' environment that can be totally exhausting. Because this relationship would be based on physicality, there is nothing here to sustain it once the initial thrill of exciting sex has worn off – which it certainly will. It can all too easily lead to the on-off-on-off situation from which people often seem unable to extricate themselves – think about Richard Burton and Elizabeth Taylor, who could not live with each other and yet were magnetically attracted to each other to the point of distraction. Once in, it can be difficult to get out...

And the moral is...

Don't take what you have read in this chapter as a *gospel truth* that is infallible – it isn't. There are far too many variables to take into account, especially since most people will exhibit parts of all three types, even though you can almost always get to recognise which one is their 'main' underlying personality. Nonetheless, it can provide you with a few clues, a 'rough guide' about what to look out for in a relationship, both as positive indicators and as warning signals. It might also give you an insight into somebody that you might not have considered even looking at before, but now you've discovered something of the 'inner man' you wonder if you might find him more appealing than you thought.

Well, there's only one way to find out...

Chapter Eight

The three women that men look for

As with Chapter Seven, it's important to understand that the first part of this chapter doesn't pretend to be an accurate depiction of the lives of early humans. It is more a narrative that illustrates why relationships can often be so difficult, from which both males and females can draw benefit.

Men frequently have a totally unreasonable expectation of how their relationships should work. It's not their fault, more it's a set of inherited instinctive responses that are actually out of date... But they don't know that.

Instincts are at the root of the problem, instincts and that insatiable quality of the male sex drive, especially during his younger years. His ancestors never had to worry about forming a relationship first, then allowing a 'respectable' amount of time before seeking to initiate sexual contact. They didn't need to worry about rejection, either, since the unfortunate females in those days probably had very little say in the matter. It's extremely unlikely that those early males ever said nonchalantly: *"Fancy an early night?"* These days, though, we live in enlightened times where a female, quite rightly, can refuse the attentions of somebody who just doesn't do it for her. But it's all new (the Marital Rape Exemption act was only repealed in 1991), and it will be many thousands of years yet before restraint becomes a *natural* part of the male sexual instinct.

So the modern male has a conflict for which there is no resolution. He knows *consciously* that he must not have sex with a female against her wishes, yet also has an inherited instinct that frequently attempts to exert its evolutionary force to bypass that conscious knowledge in order to ensure the continuance of the human race. Most males cope reasonably well with this, even if not comfortably nor always amicably, resorting to masturbatory fantasy if there is no willing female available. For some, though, once in a while, when the sex drive switch goes into the 'on' position, all other inhibitors which might prevent this most essential activity (for the survival of the species) move instantly to 'off'. He doesn't translate it like that, of course, but that's the mechanism behind the act. Interestingly, many couples experience this same suspension of responsibility during intercourse without contraception, when they decide in the heat of passion that they will just 'take a chance'.

It's a true statement that many people are caused by accidents!

But there's another problem, too, again something that the ancients didn't have to cope with... maintaining a relationship. It's the easiest way of ensuring that sex is *more likely* to be available than if he's not in one. At the beginning, anyway. The problem here is that he now has to overcome the instinct to try to mate with any female who is attractive to him as well as take an interest in the needs of his partner *outside* of any sexual activity. It's a well-known enough fact that a man is far more attentive when he wants sex than at any other time (the odd thing is, he usually has no idea just how transparent this is to females!) – it's natural then, and he doesn't have to think about it. But here he is, quite rightly in our modern society, being expected to take an interest in what she's been doing while he's been out hunting.

It's even worse if you look at class structure; then, a male has to try to find somebody within his same class structure if he is to maintain credibility. This means that a lot of the females he meets will be 'out of his class', limiting his choice. It's slightly tougher for the modern middle-class man, for his instincts will drive him towards females who look sexy while his class structure insists that he must find somebody who is 'respectable'.

Sex drive is no respecter of social class and the same instincts that sometimes encourage females to go for 'a bit of rough' will also be at *work to lure a 'respectable businessman' to commence an affair with a female who most would describe as 'a bit of a tart'. The bit of the body that people, males and females, are thinking with at these times is not at all concerned with respectability – quite the opposite, in fact. It's the uninhibited **lack** of respectability that's such a turn on!*

So the modern male, like the modern female and for all sorts of reasons, has to search for a long-term mate rather than somebody simply for a sexual coupling. He is no longer easily able to choose multiple partners (though some give it a good try!) and has to take all sorts of things into account... things like: does he actually like this female enough to commit himself totally to her? Can he cope with emotional attachment (which, as mentioned earlier, might be a purely modern phenomenon)? Can he give up the instinctive sexual pursuit of other females?

All in one

Now let's backtrack a little, because before he can answer those questions, he has to find a suitable female, an all-in-one paragon of a being who will provide sex when he wants it, look after his domestic needs, nurture him if he's wounded in battle or ill, provide him with meals for which he has 'brought home the bacon', obey his wishes, look after his young, assure him that he's the 'main man' that he already knows he is... She might be a Goddess who can work miracles – and have sex; an Earth Mother who nurtures selflessly – and has sex; or a Courtesan who always wants sex – and does the housework and nurturing as well.

Of course, she doesn't exist. He doesn't necessarily know that, though he might suspect it, which is a good thing, for it prepares him for the truth!

You might remember reading in **Chapter One** how we learn about life and living when we're very young. Well, this is no different. The male's first experience of females is his mother (it's quite different for most females, since they have far less contact with their father than with their mother, who teaches them *her* version of what males are really like) and so he expects this is how females will be. Assuming she is a 'good' mother, she will be ministering to his needs, looking after him if he's wounded, feeding him, boosting his confidence... Everything, in fact, except the sex bit. And therein lies a problem for some males, for if he learns that she doesn't like anything to do with sexuality he might well assume that *most* women don't like it, perpetuating a myth that has been passed on for many years. Of course, he might have had a negligent mother, when he'll have a whole different view of females. Either way, he'll automatically believe this is how all women are, and even if life experience shows him he's wrong, he'll still expect it to be how *most* women are.

This is why older and more experienced males often make better partners – they've had time to learn the truth about sharing life.

Anyway, for the males who are reading this book, here is some help to find the lady who will keep you happy – as long as you do your bit to keep her happy. And for the ladies reading this, you'll probably discover a useful thing or two as well.

Who's who...

In **Chapter Three** – *The way people are and the games they play,* you read about the personality types and the way they work together and you can, if you wish, use that chapter to assess with whom you might share the happiest life. Or you can read on to see more specific details about the way each female 'works' as far as a sexual relationship is concerned. Earlier, you read about the male quest for a Goddess, an Earth Mother or a Courtesan and they correspond to Warrior, Settler or Nomad, with more accent on femininity; you might be wanting to take issue with that and insist you're not looking for anything of the sort, just somebody to share your life with. Well, that's a great ideal... But the fact remains that whoever you choose will have a tendency to be mainly the Goddess, the Earth Mother or the Courtesan. She will probably reveal traits that belong to the other two from time to time but you will always be aware of that most dominant part of her personality. **Chapter Seven** – *The three men that women want* describes the Hunter, Protector and Lover, as well as the Goddess, Earth Mother and Courtesan, so we're not going to describe them again here, except for one particular type of female, which has no real counterpart in the male.

This is a combination of Earth Mother and Courtesan (**Settler** and **Nomad**.) They are quite rare, like a precious jewel, and if you find one you would be well advised to hang on to her! They are quite the most delightful people on the face of the planet – sunny disposition, warm, affectionate, supportive, nurturing... but not at all tough, so they need looking after from time to time. They'll give you the benefit of the doubt more than once but if you reject their love and affection they'll believe you no longer want them and tearfully set you free – and there'll be no going back. No matter what your own group, you can form a sound relationship with this lady as long as you respect the fact that she is easily hurt by any form of dismissiveness.

Now we'll look at how the other relationships might work – and they are this time written from the male perspective, so are subtly different from those shown in **Chapter Seven.**

The Hunter and the Goddess

This is a potential disaster though it's not impossible to make it work if you are strongly drawn to this lady sexually. You will need to be aware that you will not always have your own way, no matter how much control you try to exert or how much anger you display. If you push this lady she will simply push you back and may even manipulate you into a corner – at which she is likely to be excellent. If you like feisty females and are prepared to give a few inches as often as you try to take them, this can work. It's never going to be a peaceful and harmonious partnership though, since you will both be inclined to see challenge when there isn't any – and promptly create one as a result. There will be much in the way of a 'Will to Power' and the only real chance you have of making this a worthwhile match lies in some honest negotiation at the beginning, where you agree to talk about dissent in a controlled and respectful manner. You cannot be the overall boss here and as long as you can accept that, you have a chance of making it work. There might be better relationships for you but if this is the one you want, it's worth working at.

The Hunter and the Earth Mother

This can be wonderful as long as you genuinely enjoy being mothered. This is a lady who will want to do things for you so that she feels worthy, though she herself might not fully realise that. She will prefer you to show her – if not tell her – that you love her and will only be truly happy if she knows that you truly want her and nobody else. Being affectionate or showing emotional response might not be a strong point with you and that's about the only thing that could cause a serious problem here, so you would need, once in a while, to get past that natural inhibition and let her know she's important to you. This will make her heart sing and you will have a better life as a result. She will admire your practicality, persistence and determination but may be quietly doubtful about your tendency towards cynicism and/or scepticism. She will, though, always defend you to anybody who casts any sort of aspersion towards you, though this might be partly for her own benefit, defending her choice of mate. She will usually give in in any argument, rather than cause upset, though may sulk or do the martyr thing, which can be irritating. You'll need to just put up with that.

The Hunter and the Courtesan

This can be an excellent match because of the almost magnetic attraction that can exist between these two types. You will love her light-hearted and somewhat frivolous way of being, though you probably won't tell her that... This won't matter in the least because she'll be too busy admiring the way you can handle the problems of life, tackling them head on and winning, most of the time. Her sexiness will almost always put you 'in the mood' even when you're tired out and it's likely that she will arouse you to greater heights of passion than anybody else could. Your tendency towards a territorial attitude (jealousy, even) could cause a problem or two if you believe that other males are lusting after her. They almost certainly *will* be but you must keep it in your head that this doesn't mean she wants *them*. Start on the possessive thing and she'll put up with it for a while, maybe even enjoying it... But she'll soon feel restricted and will do what Nomads always tend to do when they feel hemmed in... move on. Accept that you will never truly know this lady even though you will think you do – she can be a bundle of surprises, some of them exasperating!

The Protector and the Goddess

Goddess she might be, practical, organised and capable in the extreme, but this is not a lady who's going to pander to your every whim and wish – and don't expect her to drop everything for sex on the spur of the moment because she doesn't work like that. She won't understand that this can make you feel unloved and there's little point in trying to explain it to her – just accept that when she has her moments she will give *most* of herself. The Goddess is far too controlled to give every part of herself, needing to retain at least some control over every situation, and it will be very easy for you to feel that she'd rather be with somebody else. This would just be you interpreting her actions as what it would mean if you were behaving the same way. She is unlikely to be the most affectionate or the sexiest female you could meet but, with a little persistence on your part, will usually be persuadable, though you should not react with evident hurt if she rejects the whole idea, which she occasionally will. At other times, she will want you just to get on with it rather than be the gentle lover, though she may or may not say so.

The Protector and the Earth Mother

This is likely to be a wishy-washy relationship that leaves you both feeling unfulfilled, unless one of you has a fair amount of Warrior or Nomad personality you can bring to bear when necessary. If not, you will soon find yourself with a humdrum life where neither of you seeks to create any excitement or variety, in your sex life or anywhere else. You might both be at ease with that but there can still be problems when confronted with some of the life difficulties that all of us experience from time to time. She will be loving and nurturing, attending to all your needs as best she can and will probably be sexually agreeable even if not especially adventurous... But she will *not* sort out anything nasty like your mum used to when you were a child (though she *will* do that for your children.) You might have been drawn to her softness; well she has that in abundance but you, as the male of the relationship, must find a way to cope with things like aggressive neighbours, financial problems, sudden emergencies and the like. She will want you to look after her in the same way that you will want her to look after you, so you might not bring out the best in each other.

The Protector and the Courtesan

The worst thing about this relationship is that you could find it overwhelming. This is a lady who is on occasions sexually demanding and may look upon the whole thing more as fun than as an expression of love. There's no doubt there will be much noisy and exhilarating passion (though some apparent Courtesans 'advertise it' but don't actually do it that well) and it is likely that your maleness will respond to that, but you might also need more expression of emotional attachment than she is likely to give. The Courtesan is a lively individual with a great sense of fun but the centre of interest in the presence of a quieter male such as you will often revert to herself. As long as you are at ease with this, there will be no great problem but if it makes you uneasy, she will definitely spot it and then will be likely to tease you rather more than you would like. She'll usually make it up to you but unless you can inject some energy of your own into the relationship she can tire of you very quickly. The biggest problem is that you have an essentially serious view of life and the world and she doesn't – and she could eventually decide that she's bored and wants to leave.

The Lover and the Goddess

This can be an excellent relationship for both of you as long as you are at ease with this lady's attempts to 'clip your wings' a little – she might find your energy irritating on occasions and will have no problem saying so. This will not mean that she's tired of *you* though, just that she needs you to calm down a bit. Secretly – for she is too control-orientated to let you know for fear it will weaken her position – she will admire your apparently inexhaustible energy (because you don't really like anybody knowing you're tired!) and sense of fun. She will probably be proud of you and the charisma that you can so easily project but will keep it to herself for fear of inflating your ego. She's unlikely to have the same level of sexual energy that is totally normal for you, and this is where arguments could arise. You will need to accept that she will reject your needs from time to time, and though if you persist she will sometimes 'give in' with a sudden bout of enthusiasm, there will be other times when it's met with a sharp rebuke. Just go along with it.

The Lover and the Earth Mother

This combination could be excellent though could just as easily be a waste of time and energy – it all depends on how much you need to able to see that you are having an impact on somebody.

Even if it's feisty attention, as with the Goddess (above) it can work well but with the Earth Mother you won't get feisty. You will get loved and nurtured, you'll get listened to and you'll get sex almost whenever you want it – possibly – but you won't know for sure whether she's enjoying it or not. It's even possible that she'll enjoy it so quietly that you're not even sure she's aware of just how spectacular you're being! If you don't like quietly sensible people who seem to always want to see the best in others, and who seem to know when you're lying or exaggerating but choose not to say anything, then this would not be a good relationship for you. If that's the case, then like it or not, you *need* someone to keep a bit of a grip on your tendency to occasional excess in all sorts of areas and who is not afraid to challenge your occasionally wild statements. Find a Goddess instead and help her to discover some of your fun in life.

The Lover and the Courtesan

You really should stay away from this one – it could be the worse relationship you could possibly experience and one from which you cannot easily escape. Angry, spiteful, confrontational, childish, wildly sexual, passionate, extreme... it will be all of those and more, unless you are exceptionally lucky. The difficulty here will come from the fact that you both will demand to be the centre of attention. If you have something that's distressing you and you try to talk about it, you are likely to get a: *"How do you think that makes me feel?"* response. There are occasional exceptions but this sort of pairing is usually based on pure physicality and neither of you have much to offer the other when that's worn off. Most of us have heard of a relationship where the couple can't live with each other or without each other and those are almost always Lover/Courtesan pairings. The physical attraction can be huge and keep calling you back with the hope that 'it'll be better this time...' But it seldom is.

The last word

None of what you have read here is 'set in stone' of course, since there are many factors that can affect a relationship, including 'chemistry'. It's possible that you will find pairings that are not recommended here and yet the couple concerned are loyal, loving and happy. But those are actually the 'exception that proves the rule' and certainly not typical. What you have read here so far is based on thousands of hours of study and can be relied upon as a source of guidance that is close to the truth.

Of course, no matter how good a relationship is, there will always be arguments, and that's where we're going next.

Chapter Nine

How to argue in a straight line – or how to avoid it in the first place

"I know you believe you understand what you think I said, but I'm not sure you realise that what you heard is not what I meant."

Think about that for a moment or two. Or longer. Then let your mind drift to some time or other when you've said something in all innocence, only to have the other person suddenly react in a very odd way indeed. What's happened is that they've interpreted what you've said according to their own internal dialogue – what it would mean if they said it, or perhaps even what it would have meant if somebody else they knew said it. Their response is totally appropriate as far as they're concerned, completely incomprehensible from your point of view. An example might help to clarify this rather odd state of affairs:

Person 1: *"I was going to have toast for my breakfast today but there's hardly any bread left."* (Meaning: 'I thought I'd better not use what's left of the bread in case we want it later.')

Person 2: (Hearing: 'If you'd bought more bread I could've had toast for my breakfast') *"Oh, don't start! You're not the only one who works hard."* (Meaning: 'I just didn't have time to go shopping.')

You can probably easily see how that little exchange could so easily go on to end up in a full-blown row. And in many relationships, it would soon escalate into stuff like where the toothpaste tube should be squeezed, spending too long on the phone, hogging the remote, whether snoring is natural, personal hygiene, navigation while driving and just about any other aspect of sharing one's life with another that you can think of. It's the way that many arguments progress and in this chapter we're going to have a look at how to 'argue in a straight line' – that is, how to have a disagreement without driving several nails into the coffin of what was once a wonderful relationship. Needless to say, personality comes into it and though we're not touching on too much of that in this chapter, it's worth noting that:

- The **Warrior** will argue to win no matter what. This is a totally natural process for them, since they cannot abide to be seen to be in the wrong. This is actually not a personality flaw – it's a genetic predisposition that you will never change. They are descended from individuals for whom making an error was a threat to survival and so an argument had to be defended to the death. The fewer people know about any error, the safer they are!

- The **Settler** will try to resolve the problem but have difficulty in expressing themselves under pressure, and an argument means far more to them that it might to either of the other two groups. They are descended from people who relied on harmony in the community for their safety, so *dis*harmony is a threat to survival. They will try their best to stand their ground but are not generally very good at it.

- The **Nomad** will argue with a great deal of noise and gesticulation, maybe even quoting all sorts of fake statistics, or 'something I heard on the telly', to back up their side of the argument. They are usually experts at 'spin' and if they sense they are on the losing end of an argument will insist that you've completely misunderstood the whole point of what they're saying, then repeat their stance... Except it will be different from the one they started with!

There are only two 'golden rules' of arguing and if you can stay with them you won't end up needing to get a divorce! The rules are: (1) Keep to the subject of whatever started the argument in the first place; and (2) Begin every sentence with 'I' or 'We', avoiding 'You' as far as you possibly can. Yes, it's difficult to keep to those rules when tempers rise but all that happens otherwise is that the argument then gets worse instead of ending with an agreement. Of course, even a saint couldn't stick to them all the time but the most important one is the first – keep to whatever the disagreement was about in the first place. Once the argument descends to the point where the argument is about the argument, there can never be a 'winner'... only two losers, because the original cause of the row has not been resolved.

Inevitably, the focus of the disagreement will shift but since you're reading this, try to stay on track and in control of things. We'll make that first in the investigation of 'Argumentese' that we're going to look at now.

Staying focussed

When an argument has come down to the point where we are simply trying to win, something odd happens. We lose sight of trying to solve the problem (which is often based on the sort of misunderstanding illustrated earlier) and instead seek to demonstrate that we are better/smarter/sharper than our 'opponent'. That won't change their mind about anything, and all that happens instead is that we strengthen their resolve to win. Then, when we cannot find a suitable clever response in time to maintain our position, our subconscious does something very obliging... It puts an entirely different argument in our mind so that we can start again from a level footing. Put simply, it's a cop-out because we perceive we might be losing the original battle, so we start a new one. Our argument partner will usually take the bait, and before we know it we're into nothing more useful than a shouting match from which it's difficult to extricate ourselves without either stomping off to escape, or indulging in passive-aggressive silence. This all hinges around a basic fact:

When somebody has taken a position in an argument, they will do anything to avoid changing it. Especially the Warrior...

As long as one person can stay focussed though, things can be a lot more constructive. When the conflict starts to drift into other concepts, there are many possible responses:

Bad: *"Just keep to the point! You always try to..."* This has just become part of the 'point-scoring' process.

Bad: *"Oh that's right! Dig all that stuff up again!"* Defensive posturing, designed to stop them going into some place where you feel at fault.

Bad: *"What on earth are you talking about now? Stop trying to change the subject and try to keep up!"* More point-scoring and hugely inflammatory!

This won't improve things at all... There are many other 'bad' responses but you get the idea. On the other hand:

Good: *"Okay... but can we try to keep to the point? I really want to sort this out so we don't get into another argument about it later on."* If this is delivered reasonably calmly, it's difficult for anybody to disagree without looking a bit silly!

Tip: If you recognise that there's been a misunderstanding, don't fight back! Instead, do something like putting both hands up and saying: *"Oh, sorry, I didn't put that very well, did I? What I meant was..."* Then, of course, explain again what you were trying to say the first time. If you rankle a bit at that, then consider this: if you created the misunderstanding, it should be you who resolves it!

The 'I' process

Once an argument is under way, damage limitation is always a good thing. Scoring points might make you feel good temporarily but what it does to a relationship doesn't lead to long-term happiness. Personal insults rank amongst the most damaging of elements in an argument and if you can avoid them as far as possible, this can only be a good thing. It's actually not difficult if you remember to start every sentence, as far as possible, with 'I', rather than 'You'. The spat out: *"You make me sick!"* for instance, is peculiarly pointless (it also gives power to your partner – see later) and achieves nothing other than invite the other person to come back with a suitable retort. It can even escalate into the *"Well, perhaps you'd be better off if I wasn't around then!"* Not a problem if that's what you were after, not so good if you were just trying to score points, because now you have only: *"That's right, that's your answer to everything isn't it?";* *"Well, that's entirely up to you.";* *"Yes, that's probably a good idea!"* Those are the sort of responses you might give to show that you won't be threatened, of course, and are an attempt to regain control. The alternative is the rather lame statement similar to: *"Well, I'm not saying that..."* Best to avoid the situation in the first place, then.

Beginning every new 'point' in the argument with 'I' or 'We' means that it's very difficult to hurl an insult that might get you what you *don't* want and much easier to explain how you actually feel. There are a few good ways of avoiding escalation, or 'rewinding' a little if things have already got a bit out of hand:

- *"I feel upset when we get like this..."* (Much better than 'You make me sick!')
- *"I don't want us to carry on fighting..."* (Instead of: 'Shut the **** up!')
- *"We've got ourselves on opposite sides of the fence here..."*
- *"We're doing it again – can you help me sort us out?"*
- *"I want to make us ok but I don't know how."*
- *"We've got ourselves into a bit of a state here, haven't we? I hate this."*

You get the idea. Most people really don't want their rows to end in a break up or even lead a few steps towards it, though there are few who feel no regret after a big 'bust up' (though that's a situation we will be looking at later in the book). Keeping that in mind allows you to avoid much of the response associated with retaliation, deliberate challenge, demonstration of superiority, sarcasm, personal insults and the like. And it's far easier to keep those things close to the surface if you practise the 'I' and 'We' idea in any argument.

Tip: when you realise that your partner is doing their best to hurt, insult or otherwise challenge you, a totally disarming approach is: *"What are you trying to make me feel?"* Asking that question will normally calm the situation... But if you get an unfavourable answer, your relationship might be in more trouble than you thought. In which case there's help for that later, in **Chapter Eleven** – *When it all goes wrong.*

Bullying

You might be able to get your own way by bullying your partner into submission – screaming, shouting, threatening, ridiculing and generally abusing... But you do have to ask yourself an important question: *"Why am I in this relationship and what good do I get out of it?"* You can ask yourself the same question if you're on the receiving end of such behaviour, too, though there's a whole section later on – again in **Chapter Eleven** – on dealing with an abusive partner.

If you just don't seem to be able to stop bullying your partner even though you genuinely want to be with them, it's important to recognise that you have a problem with self-worth and self-esteem. You might want to argue about that but when you think about it, why else would you feel the need to use force? If you believed you were worthy of whatever you are trying to achieve, you would not need to shout about it. And if you believe your partner simply doesn't respect you enough, so that you have to resort to emotional pressure, then again, why are you in that relationship? Where's the joy?

If you know you've been a bully but genuinely want to save

your relationship it is vital that you:

- Seek professional help to deal with your problem – and be honest with the therapist, otherwise they can't help you. The **Resources** section at the back of the book lists some useful contacts.
- Ask your partner to help you get better. This can be difficult if you've been abusive to them because you might feel awkward and they could refuse.

Although you might find yourself resisting this course of action, it's an essential process for you, because even if you can't save this relationship, you'll be better equipped to handle the next one properly.

Tip: If you admit to yourself that you've been a bully and decide to make changes in your life, however you do it, it will take your partner quite a while to trust the 'new you'. Ask for their help, which will involve them in your recovery and speed the process up, as well as make it more likely that you will not lose them.

Trap setting

This is usually more the domain of the female rather than the male, and an example of the age-old 'battle of the sexes'. There are two styles of trap that are commonly laid – the deliberate tripwire and the omission. The worst thing is that the male has no idea he's fallen into one even after it's been sprung! And when he asks his lady what's wrong, she is inclined to come back with that: *"If you don't know, I'm not going to tell you..."* response.

The **tripwire** is where something has been contrived to test an idea or belief that has presented itself to the female mind for whatever reason. For instance, the female believes her partner has a secret girlfriend and resolves to find out. The 'tripwire' is the information that she has to go and visit a sick relative for a few days, in the belief that as soon as she's out of the way he will be visiting his girlfriend – or she'll be visiting him. Of course, she comes home earlier than she said, expecting – hoping, even – to find him with his girlfriend. Either that or absent so she can sit and wait for his arrival and gloat at his discomfort before pitching into a triumphal row.

The **omission trap** is keeping quiet about an approaching birthday or anniversary to see if he remembers... And if he doesn't then she can flounce around in an aggrieved state, dropping hints, until it dawns on him and he is full of guilt.

If you have a tendency toward this sort of behaviour pattern, ask yourself why, if you love this man, you want to set a trap in the first place and why you are so triumphant when it's sprung. If you love somebody, why would you want to make them feel bad? There's only one plausible reason and that is if you've already decided he's 'guilty' and want to catch him out. The problem is that when he avoids the trap, you might simply decide that he's being sneakily clever and resolve to set a better trap next time. Ultimately, if you continue, this will end in disaster as you lose all positive emotional response towards him because of the erroneous belief that he's in some way tricking you.

Tip: if you think your partner might miss your birthday/anniversary, why not say, a couple of weeks in advance, something like: *"Have you bought my card yet?"* If he hasn't, he soon will! You might believe he should remember anyway, and there's a truth there. But it's worth the thought that females have always had to remember dates and have an inbuilt calendar so they are naturally better at it.

Irrational jealousy

Irrational jealousy – that is, jealousy with no sound reason for its existence – is one of the most destructive forces in any relationship. It can lead to rows, heartache, divorce... even murder. Probably the hardest thing to understand is that the problem usually has more to do with the person experiencing jealousy than it does their partner. When there are grounds for the emotion, this might not be the case but we're talking here about the situation where it flares up for no good reason at all. We'll look at two quite different examples, the first one probably the most obvious.

1 Somebody gets it into their head that their partner is likely to have an affair with somebody else. Because there is no evidence of this, they begin to investigate more and more intensely, maybe following their partner themselves or perhaps even hiring somebody to do so. This obsession – for that is what it is – can never be relieved because the longer the feeling lasts, the more convinced the jealous one becomes that they are somehow having the wool pulled over their eyes. It can escalate to ridiculous proportions of extreme possessiveness until the partner eventually has had enough of the whole thing and decides to either create something to be jealous of... or walk.

2 Somebody fears for no good reason that their partner is more popular than they themselves are, that their joint friends like them more, that they are favoured by both sets of relatives, that others believe the jealous one to be in some way inferior... this can so easily lead to sniping and/or attempts to ridicule the partner privately and in front of others so that they can see the 'truth' about this person whom they think is so wonderful. Eventually, people begin to take notice of it all... But they don't see what was intended – instead they see a nasty, sniping individual behaving badly towards their partner. Then, what that person feared becomes truth...

In both the above cases, the problem lies in the mind and thought processes of the person who is jealous and has absolutely nothing to do with the person they are jealous *of*. It's easy to see that here, in print, but it feels *totally real* to the person suffering the jealousy problem. In the first case, the jealous person believed that just about everybody else in the world was going to be more desirable to their partner than they were... otherwise they would not be so convinced that they had to keep such a close rein on them. It *feels* like it's the partner's behaviour causing it when it happens but that's just our subconscious ego-protection systems at work. It's difficult when we really want somebody and we feel they might leave, but it's worth remembering that there's absolutely no point in trying to keep somebody with you who doesn't want to stay. It's a recipe for misery.

In the second case, the emotional 'driver' is different. Here, it's the fear that the jealous individual is being shown up as 'not all that' and so that ego-protection creation creates the urge to suppress this 'evidence'. But again, there's no point. You can't make somebody 'unclever' – all you can do is show yourself up by trying!

Tip: if you find yourself struggling with feelings of jealousy, before taking any action of any sort, write down your fears and what it is that's creating them on a fresh sheet of paper. When you've finished, ask yourself: if this was a film plot would viewers 'get it' or would they wonder if somebody had missed something out? Would they be on your side or your partner's? And take notice of the answer...

And finally...

We'll finish this chapter with a look at two ideas which are not actually a part of 'argumentese' but are nonetheless of enormous importance in relationships. The first one is the belief that your partner 'makes' you miserable when they should 'make' you happy. Well, the truth is that nobody can *make* you feel anything you don't want to feel. Anything you experience is based on *your* reactions to what is going on around and within you and nobody can change that. If you believe somebody has made you happy, it simply means that your reaction – **your reaction** – to what they are doing or saying is to feel happy. It might create totally different feelings in somebody else. Irritation perhaps. Sadness maybe.

This idea is easy to understand if you recognise that there isn't a single joke in the world that makes *everybody* laugh; there's not a single book or film that makes *everybody* sad; and there's not a single song or tune that makes *everybody* like it. So anything your partner does would create different responses in different people, and those responses would depend on everything that had happened in their life. Try this idea: if somebody you really detested said to you something like: *"I'm going to MAKE you love me,"* would they have much chance of success? Of course not!

There's more to this. Whenever you say something like: *"You make me sick!"* to anybody, you are telling them they have power over you, that they can interfere with the very core of your being. It's not much of an insult, is it? And if you want to play one of the ultimate mind games with somebody who says something like that to you, you can smile and say: *"Thank you!"* They may or may not understand it – but it'll make you feel better!

The second concept we're going to explore is that of compromise. It's a necessary part of every successful relationship but most people don't get it quite right. We'll look at two examples of conflict and provide a workable solution for each that doesn't leave either one feel compromised.

Example 1. Jack squeezes the toothpaste tube in the middle because he knows that's why it's designed as a squeezy tube instead of something more rigid. Jill, though, always squeezes it from the end because she knows it's designed to avoid waste. She gets fed up with having to straighten the tube out every time while Jack is irritated that Jill keeps going on about it. The compromise is to buy toothpaste in a pump dispenser. (Or perhaps buy two tubes of toothpaste, one each, but that's not really a compromise!)

Example 2. Anne wants to have a pub meal in the local High Street because it's within walking distance. Linda wants to go to the swishy wine bar she's been told about but it's two miles away and they'll have to get a bus. The compromise is to go somewhere entirely different this time that they can both agree on and then talk about when they'll try out the new wine bar.

It's not always easy to avoid an argument; it's not always easy to patch things up after there's been one. But it can help a lot if you manage to keep in mind that your partner's feelings are every bit as valid as yours, even if you feel differently from each other. The truth is, as has already been mentioned (and will be mentioned again later!) none of us can actually *control what we feel*, only what we do with it after we've felt it.

And there's more about that later on.

Chapter Ten

Making a poor thing better

*Most people won't need to do **everything** that's is covered in this chapter and even those that think they will are likely to discover that when they've done some of it, the rest just happens automatically. It doesn't take account of the presence of children or other family members so some adjustment might be needed here and there.*

In this chapter, we're going to have a look at how you might be able to renovate an ailing relationship to the point where you vividly remember, with a surge of happiness, why you got into it in the first place. We're not talking about when everything has collapsed to the point where you no longer even speak because you detest each other (that's covered later) but of the situation where you no longer bother to try to please each other, and life has assumed that 'same old, same old' quality.

Usually, this has happened gradually over a period of years, so gradually that it's a while before you notice it... And when you do, you're so used to it that it seems 'normal', especially when your partner seems unconcerned, saying nothing untoward. The truth, though, is that they probably are saying nothing for the very same reason – *their* partner (you!) seems unconcerned. You're not unhappy together, but then again, you're not ecstatically happy either. You don't want to break up but you'd be hard pressed to speak with conviction about what it is in the relationship that makes you want to be together. Familiarity, perhaps. Security, maybe. But wasn't it something more exhilarating in the very beginning?

If it was ever good in the first place, it can be made so again!

You might not rediscover that first flush of excitement that comes with a new relationship (though it's not impossible); it's not always possible to recreate the strength of sexual desire that you would sometimes feel for an entire day in the beginning, just waiting for the evening... But you can certainly restore things to the point that you're pleased to hear the key in the lock, or to be back home with your partner instead of just pleased to be back home.

Before we set about this somewhat daunting task, let's have a look at the sort of relatively simple things that make a relationship work, as opposed to just exist:

- Talking to each other (instead of just passing a comment occasionally.)
- Laughing together (even if your sense of humour doesn't match.)
- Sharing a meal (instead of just eating at the same time.)
- Deliberate eye contact (instead of just a glance.)
- Purposely touching each other.
- Making each other feel good.
- Sex.

Now, for an exercise, score each of those elements for their current quality on a scale of 1 – 10 where '10' is excellent and '1' is almost non existent. Add up the total. Now cast your mind back to a short while after you became a genuine 'item' and do the same evaluation. If the totals are close, within 10% say, then you can probably skip this chapter! On the other hand, if there is a distinct difference, ask yourself this question: *if, back then, things had been as they are now, would you think this was a good relationship?* If the answer is 'yes' then you're easily pleased and, again, you can skip the rest of this chapter.

So, you're still here. Okay, let's get to work. Those things in the list aren't presented in any particular order of importance, except for Sex, which is potentially the most difficult area to repair. We'll get onto them all later but we first have to take account of something that can easily get in the way of the entire reconstruction project.

Bus stop syndrome

The 'bus stop syndrome' really refers to a rather strange human process of unintentional habituation and is best illustrated by an imaginary situation:

Pretend that you've moved to a new area. Today is Monday, your first day of travelling to your workplace from here and you walk to the bus stop at the top of your road. There are a few people there when you arrive, a couple who are together, and three others who don't seem to know each other. Because you don't know any of them and they take no notice of you, you don't speak. You all get on the bus when it arrives and you notice the couple and one of the others get off at the stop before yours.

The next day, the same people are at the bus stop. The couple and one of the others get off at their stop, as you had anticipated... The same thing happens on the Wednesday, Thursday and Friday and you now know these people by sight, of course. The weekend passes and it's back to work on Monday morning. You walk up to the bus stop and the same people are there... Now: if you don't speak to them this day, you probably never will!

The reason, of course, is that you've already shown them that you don't talk to strangers and they've shown you the same thing. If you were to start talking to them now, they might think it a bit odd – or worse, ignore you, so that you start to feel uncomfortable. And after another couple of weeks have gone by, that unintentional habituation is now so deeply entrenched it has become 'normal'. Just like your relationship. It becomes increasingly difficult to act 'out of character'... Just like your relationship.

But that's not the end of our little story! It continues:

One morning, the bus fails to stop, sailing straight past and continuing up the road, disappearing into the distance. Everybody looks at each other in disbelief. "Now what?" one says in exasperation. "I've got an important meeting first thing!" One half of the couple groans. "You're lucky! I'm done for... My boss has already had a go at me for being one minute late every day!" Another person shakes her head. "What on earth was the driver thinking?" You smile. "This is not a regular occurrence then?" Everybody choruses: "No! Never known it before." One of them smiles in your direction: You're new to the area, aren't you?" You agree, easily dropping into conversation about what time the next bus is likely to arrive.

The next morning, you walk up to the bus stop as usual and the same people are there as usual. They smile in your direction, one says: "Good morning!" and you recognise, somewhere deep inside you, that a new habit is just starting to form...

Of course, it was common ground, the shared unusual experience that allowed them to break the spell. The bus failing to stop was not part of the usual routine at all and so they could all move outside their usual habituation. So all you have to do to get started on the relationship repair is to discover or create something that is not part of the normal 'fabric' of your everyday life together. It *can* feel a little difficult at first but once you've got the ball rolling and your partner joining in, it gets progressively easier.

If you decide to wait for something to happen, you could wait a very long time. As long as for that bus to not stop when it should have, perhaps. So rather than wait, you can set about creating something yourself. It's actually not that difficult and we'll have a look at some examples:

- Send yourself a large bouquet of flowers to be delivered when you're both at home. When they arrive, you can both be intrigued by the mystery, trying to work out who might have sent them and why, especially if you have the florist enclose a cryptic message. Insist they must have come from your partner and that you think it's a really nice thing to have done.

- If you have the devil in you, send your partner the flowers instead – anonymously of course. The conversation could be quite interesting!
- Anonymously send yourself two tickets for the theatre, making sure they're for the best seats. Ask your partner to find out what the play is about.
- This one's expensive, but good: book a weekend away at a swishy hotel and claim it's a competition prize. Talk about how the only good thing you've ever won before is your partner.

All the above, and other things like them, perform a specific task – they provide an excuse to behave differently, to change something. Remember, you only have to break that habituation, and do it as naturally as you can; it sets up a special situation in the mind where other unusual things are far more readily acceptable as being 'natural' under the circumstances. Once started, you only have to profess enjoyment at sharing the event with your partner and the rest becomes steadily easier. If your partner will accept sudden change joyfully – and many people will – you can mend things far faster than you ever thought possible.

*Now, there is one thing that can throw a spanner in the works and that is if your partner simply refuses to respond, maybe even becoming irritated by it. Well, if that happens, your relationship was in a worse state than you realised and you will need the help you can find in Chapters Eleven, Twelve or Fourteen. It's not a time for recriminations – your partner cannot choose their feelings (or lack of feelings) and it doesn't mean all is lost unless **they** say so. It just means you have a tougher task than you thought.*

This leads us on to something else that's important – knowing when to give in, give up, or get out. There's no way that anybody else can give you clear information about knowing when to exercise any of those options because it depends entirely on how you function and the personality type of your partner. If you are by nature a patient person (and probably a **Settler**) than you will put up with a bit more trouble getting a response from your partner than if you were a **Nomad** or a **Warrior**. Be guided by how you feel. If you find yourself feeling totally fed up with making the effort for no response, or even evident interest from your partner, that's probably time to give up... And you might want to ask yourself if it's time to get out. Only you can decide, and there's help for you in **Chapter Fourteen** – *A trick or two to deal with a break up* if you think it is. And what about 'giving in?' Well, there are two reasons why that might be the answer:

1 You've made the effort and nothing much has changed except for the fact that your partner has indicated they're not too keen on all this new stuff that keeps on happening. They just want things to jog along like they've been doing. You love them and so you give in...

2 You've been on the other end of somebody creating surprises, buying you flowers, winning holiday weekends in competitions and all sorts of stuff and you've been resisting making a positive response for one reason or another. But you realise that if they're doing all this, resistance is futile... And so you give in.

Anyway, now we're going to investigate how to work at each of those seven important aspects of your relationship one-by-one. Here's a reminder:

• Talking to each other (instead of just passing a comment occasionally.)
• Laughing together (even if your sense of humour doesn't match.)
• Sharing a meal (instead of just eating at the same time.)

- Deliberate eye contact (instead of just a glance.)
- Purposely touching each other.
- Purposely making each other feel good.
- Sex.

Talking to each other

More precisely, this should be 'having a conversation'. This is not the same thing at all as just talking after your partner has said something, or passing a comment about something on the television or in the newspaper. Conversation is the major form of communication in humans since it includes 'NVC' (Non Verbal Communication) in the form of body language and the tiny expressions that flit across our features as we react to what we are hearing and experiencing – they're called 'micro expressions' and some people react as strongly to them as they do the spoken word.

People who converse more with each other are automatically sharing more of their lives with each other. Proper conversation includes smiles and grins, nods, shrugs, headshakes, hand movements, eyebrow movement, eye contact and head movement... and the other person cannot but begin to resonate with these things. They tell us subconsciously a great deal about how we are being perceived and the effect we might be having, allowing us to adjust our conversation accordingly. We all do it, even if we don't notice it. We all *read* it even if we don't notice it. When you're trying to get back into the habit of conversation after it has been lost, it can take a while to get used to it, longer still for it to feel natural.

The best way to start is to ask a question then *listen* to the answer so that you can carry things on. You won't make it happen all at once; be content at first with getting any exchange going where you are actually taking notice of each other and discussing something, rather than just passing a comment or two. Yes, it might seem a bit stilted at first, if you're out of the habit, and your partner will probably notice... But what's wrong with that? Talk about something on the television, something you've seen in the newspaper or even on the bus, train, or your drive to work or the shops. BUT don't just talk! Stop to listen to the reply and when you stop, keep eye contact and look interested. You can even stop without finishing your story so your partner is encouraged to say something like: *"Well, what happened then?"*

Your partner's personality is important for this one:

- The **Warrior** is not naturally a conversationalist and may not respond very much. This would be totally normal for them. They'll soon shut you up if they get bored, which might mean giving up, giving in, or deciding to get out.
- The **Settler** enjoys conversation and will usually be eager to join in... They might be anxiously curious (wondering what you're leading up to) or peculiarly 'clingy'. It will pass.
- The **Nomad** will usually get into the spirit of things and will probably end up talking about themselves. This is an essential part of a relationship with this personality type.

Laughing together

Sharing laughter is almost as important as sharing conversation and often a lot easier, too. You don't have to engineer anything here – which is particularly difficult in any case – because all that's necessary is to join in when your partner laughs at something. It is important that you understand why they're laughing, even if it doesn't really amuse *you* very much, otherwise you can get into the awful situation where you're asked what's funny. While you're laughing, look at your partner; eye contact always creates or enhances sensations of 'togetherness'. Even if they don't return your look, they will be aware of it.

Sharing a meal

One of the problem areas these days is eating, which is so often on a tray sitting in front of the television. There's nothing particularly wrong with that – when the relationship is sound. Otherwise, it can serve to increase the 'solitariness' of each half of the couple, since all that is happening then is that you are eating at the same time. Not at all the same thing as sharing a meal.

It can be difficult – and feel awkward – to suddenly start eating at the table again, although that could well be the subject of a shared conversation, of course. It's easy enough to instigate: *"I've made a special meal,"* (and if you use this you should have) *"So shall we sit at the table for a change?"* If you're not the cook in the household, then a different approach will be needed: *"Special treat tonight – I've booked us a table at..."* and make sure the restaurant is a good one. This will often trigger questions such as: *"What's all this in aid of?"* to which there is only one answer, that must be delivered with a smile: *"Well, us, actually. I've been thinking we should do more together."*

You can probably already see that this a potentially extremely powerful way of getting your relationship back on track, since it is likely to lead into shared conversation, shared laughter and eye contact. This is all a lot easier when there is nothing to cause distraction or attract attention, such as the television or some domestic thing that has to be attended to. It's a little more obvious than simply sharing laughter or conversation as discussed previously but this shouldn't present a problem unless your partner is particularly unresponsive.

Deliberate eye contact

This is common in a new relationship and, indeed, most people go out of their way to find it, and they usually revel in it. But as we get used to one another, it tends to diminish until it's just the occasional cursory glance. *You cannot re-establish a close relationship without getting back into the habit of eye contact.* The easiest way to do this is during conversation, when it will seem completely normal, and you might now be beginning to realise how integrated all these elements are. Sharing a meal provides the perfect opportunity for conversation, shared laughter, and eye contact, as well as the other things on the list. Even sex, for that's something that can follow an evening out far more naturally and romantically than an evening in front of the television.

- **If you're male:** *don't give any indication that you* **expect** *sex to be part of the menu. Make overtures by all means but accept the situation gracefully if they're refused.*
- **If you're female:** *be aware that your partner is likely to be* **hoping** *that sex will be available for 'afters' but this doesn't mean you have to go along with it.*

Deliberate eye contact can be flirtatious or challenging... Flirtatious is probably best, in the context of what this chapter is about!

Touching each other

This can be as simple as holding hands, trailing your fingers along your partner's shoulders as you pass by, just a light touch in a non-sexual area that's sustained long enough to ensure that it's recognised as not an accident, or just placing your hand on the back of your partner's hand for a moment while you are sitting at a meal table. More integration here, as you can see.

Purposely making each other feel good

This is both one of the easiest things and the most difficult of things to do! Easy, because we all like to feel good; difficult if the 'bus stop syndrome' has led you away from the habit. It's easy to make the mistake of doing something that you think will make your partner feel good but failing to let them know that you did it for that very reason. If trying to please them is not something you do any more, they won't know unless you tell them. So it needs to be something obvious, something that simply cannot be misunderstood. Here's a small list of things:

Sending flowers with a message; writing a special card and leaving it for them to find; arranging a special treat concerning something you know they like; leaving a nice hand-written note (not typed, nor a text or email!) *for them to find when you're not there; leaving a single rose on their pillow.*

The important thing about all of those is the message that you must make sure goes with them: *I Love You Still* is good, as is: *I don't tell you often enough that I care* or: *You are still the most important thing in my life.* Maybe you think those sentiments are a bit 'slushy'... But what would you feel like to be on the receiving end? Whatever you do should encourage your partner to respond but this is another situation where personality comes into it:

- The **Warrior** might not show much at the time but probably will later.
- The **Settler** is likely to be evidently moved and respond immediately.
- The **Nomad** will either laugh or respond enthusiastically. Either is good.

This particular element can so easily work as a cure for 'bus stop syndrome' and lead to any of the other elements in our list, and once again you can see how things can blend together so well.

Sex

This is probably the most difficult thing to re-establish if it has been absent for a while. It's such a profound behaviour and there's no way of approaching it delicately – sexual intercourse is many wonderful things but not one of them is delicate! Not if the sex is any good, anyway. So conversation about it is important. If it has been absent in your relationship for a while, then it's best to concentrate on the other six elements in our list before even *thinking* about getting sex working again. Trying to get to it too quickly risks making it seem sordid or embarrassing, or worse still, as if that was all you were after. It could even wreck the whole project of getting your relationship back on track. So if your relationship is in a *very* bad way, here's a good plan to follow:

- Read everything in this book again, starting at **Chapter One** and understanding some of that early learning about relationships.
- Be sure you take your partner's personality group into account.
- Get rid of any 'unsexy' behaviour patterns.
- Do everything in this chapter but don't rush.
- Remember that if you talk to a man about sex, he usually wants to do it immediately – this is just the way the male is made – so leave that bit until last!

That should rescue even the most stagnant of relationships. But on the other hand, if things have just been getting a bit humdrum lately and you only need to inject a bit more of a 'zing' into your life together, you can go for the quick fix:

- Book a table in an expensive restaurant – but do make sure you both like the type of cuisine.
- Wear something you know flatters you but also which you know your partner likes. If you don't know for sure, ask what they think you look best in.
- If you're male, arrange for roses to be at the table (if she like roses, of course – other flowers can do almost as well.)

- Deliberate over the menu, talking about what you might eat and drink.
- Make frequent eye contact with smiles.
- Go for a lot of flirting and a little alcohol – not the other way round!
- Touch your partner's hand and tell them you love them.
- If you're female, tell him you're not wearing any knickers.
- If you're male, tell her she is an absolutely sexily stunning lady.

It's not a foolproof plan but unless your relationship has deteriorated to the point where you feel awkward or foolish at the idea of trying to follow it, it will work far more often than not. And if something goes wrong with any part of it, especially the sex, accept it with good grace... because at least you've started the process and it's something you did together.

There's more about sexual difficulties in **Chapter Sixteen** *– Common problems, uncommon answers.*

Chapter Eleven

When it all goes wrong

When a relationship fails it's usually the case that it fails more from one side than the other. You're either the one to do the dumping or the one to be dumped. In this chapter, we look at how best to handle both situations.

There is no such thing as the perfect relationship, no matter how certain you are at the beginning that you've found one. People change and things that were once endearing become an irritant, the husky voice becomes a rasp and those little quirky attitudes about completely normal things become neurotic nonsense. Or perhaps it's something a bit darker. That endearing wish to always want to be with you becomes possessiveness, the assertiveness you once admired has turned into bullying abuse, and that odd little sexual peccadillo has become downright disgustingly crude and obnoxious.

Or maybe there's no real accounting for what has gone wrong at all. All you know is the practical and down-to-earth **Warrior** who could take charge of any difficult situation has become a crushingly boring control freak; the gentle and loving **Settler** has turned into a wet weekend; or that vibrant and charismatic **Nomad** has somehow turned into a raging narcissist with no thought for anybody but themselves. Maybe it's not *that* bad yet but you know only too well that it's not going to work – you don't even *want* it to work any more – and it's about time you moved on. On the other hand, it might be the case that things have become so unbearable that the person you used to want to be near all the time now makes your skin creep if they so much as look at you.

It's over, but you're still there. You've not addressed it yet.

For most people, it's not an easy task to tell somebody you just don't want to be with them any more, though it's fair to say that females often appear to handle it better than males. Males will often, in fact, behave badly enough for long enough that the female takes charge and gives him his marching orders. This is probably because of his fear that she will start crying if he tries to end it, something he finds difficult to cope with. He can easily feel like a bully. On the other hand, when a female tells the male it's over and *he* starts crying (not unknown) she will probably groan inwardly and give him the *'It's not you, it's me, you're a lovely guy'* speech, with the assurance that he'll soon be snapped up by somebody more appreciative of him. Then she escapes before he gets into begging mode because that's what *she* finds difficult to deal with.

But now we're going to rewind a little, because most people agonise for ages before finally managing to psych themselves up enough to attempt 'the deed'. There are four main reasons for this, all based on fear:

- Fear of an abusive partner
- Fear of hurting the partner
- Fear of what others might think
- Fear they're doing the 'wrong thing'

It could even be a combination of two or more of these situations but we'll look at each, and how to deal with them, separately.

The abusive partner

It's easy to imagine that an abusive partner is necessarily male, but for some time now, there have been almost as many abused men as there are abused women. The abuse can be physical or emotional, of course, and though most people have more overt fear of physical violence, it's emotional and psychological abuse that will cause the most profound and long-lasting damage. If it's suffered for a long enough period of time, the victim can come to truly believe whatever they've been told about themselves. This can sometimes be worse for males, for they are less likely to discuss it with others and therefore less likely to find support that might help them deal with the situation. Once the abusive behaviour has started, it's fair to say that the relationship is over, save for an extremely rare circumstance which we will look at in detail in the next chapter. For the moment, though, just accept that whether the abuse is physical or emotional, it's time to get out. Not to try, but to do it, whatever it takes.

There's no point in trying to reason with an abuser – they simply turn whatever your approach is into a weapon for more of the same, either physical or emotional. Also, it's pointless trying to appeal to their decent side for the same reasons. Usually, they've suffered abuse themselves in their younger years, which is where and how they've learnt how to do it. This is the way, of course, that we learn everything about human interaction and you now know how difficult it is to start behaving differently. Although they will almost never realise it, they are acting out of fear themselves and seeking to create fear, since they've learnt that's the best way to control others. 'Do it to them so they can't do it to you' is the maxim by which they live, and any attempts to reason with them are seen, in their subconscious, as seeking to rob them of their personal power. It's possible that couples' counselling or anger-management sessions can make a difference but they have to *genuinely* be willing to go through the therapy (there's more about that in another chapter) and most aren't.

So, the **only** reliable way to deal with this situation is to get out of it as quickly and as quietly as you can. No discussions. Find yourself somewhere to live, pack your bags when the abuser isn't about and *go.* If that's not possible for any reason, you might have to leave your belongings behind and manage as best you can with the help of friends, family or even officialdom (see the 'Resources' section at the end of this book). Yes, it will be tough and you will feel a mixture of guilt, fear, regret and all sorts of other uncomfortable responses, both emotional and physical. It *will* pass, and the most important thing to keep in mind to help you through the storm is that it would definitely not have got any better if you'd stayed.

In the next chapter, you will see that, once in a while, an abuser changes dramatically; this is the result of a complex psychological process that occurs deep in the subconscious. But since the abuse process is actually being fed by the continued existence of the relationship, this won't happen while the couple are still together, so you still only have one sensible course of action: leave ASAP.

Hurting the partner

If this is what keeps you in a relationship that's finished as far as you're concerned, then your fear that you might hurt your partner is not only totally justified – you're already doing it. Do you truly believe that they haven't noticed that something's not right? Are you able to convince yourself that they are so unaware of problems that they are as happy as they could ever be? 'Probably not' is likely to be the honest answer to both questions, unless you are the consummate actor... and that's even worse. It's worse, because at some point, you're going to drop the bombshell on them that it's over – unless you've already decided to sacrifice your own happiness for theirs, and have vowed to make sure they will go to their grave believing that you loved them until the end.

You might manage that for a while of course, or at least until one of those monstrous surges of animal attraction to another makes itself felt. Then, of course, it's only a matter of time. The point is that you're either already hurting your partner because they know that something is far from the way it should be, or you're building up an even bigger head of steam with which to devastate them later; once you know inside yourself that it's over, it's unfair to cause more hurt than necessary. Of course it's not easy telling somebody you don't want to be with them any more but it's not something you need to feel guilty about. Feelings change and we are not in charge of how our emotions and sexual desires alter over a period of time. Sometimes people hope that if they sit it out it will get better – and sometimes that happens. The problem is, it usually doesn't last.

We are only with people in the first place because there is a reciprocal attraction. When those feelings fade for one half of the couple, the relationship is finished and it's cruel to continue with it. Not only are you preventing the other person from finding happiness with somebody else, but you are also inhibiting your own chances of finding the person you will want to spend your life with. So, your task is to take a deep breath and say something. In these circumstances, *"We need to talk..."* is a *good* 'opener', for it gives a bit of a warning that will cushion the blow, even if only ever so slightly.

What others might think

Of all the reasons to stay in a worn-out relationship when you really want out, this one is the dumbest! No matter what others think about you leaving, it won't change the way you feel about your partner. If somebody says: *"Are you mad, or what?"* all it tells you is what *they* feel – but you *don't* feel like that and it's your relationship so their thoughts are totally invalid. If, instead, they say something like: *"Well, it's about time!"* all that tells you is that they didn't think much of your partner in the first place. But you did, so their thoughts are invalid. And if they say: *"Oh, no! I thought you two were set for life!"* all that tells you is that either they're unobservant or you're good at keeping your feelings private. But it was never them who were going to spend their life with your partner – it was you. So, again, their thoughts are completely invalid. Whatever anybody else does or does not

think, and even if they give the impression that they reckon you're the 'bad guy', you already know that it's not enough to make you want to stay with the same partner. In fact, in this circumstance it's not so much the difficulty of breaking up that's holding you back but anxiety about how *you* will feel about what *they* think when you do it. Well, whenever you do it you will probably feel the same, so you might as well get it over with...
"We need to talk..."

Doing the 'wrong thing'

This is an interesting and totally unhelpful situation! If you want to get out, then whether or not it's the 'wrong thing' by some odd criterion or other is completely immaterial. It's not working, you're not enjoying it, and that's the end of it. Usually, there are several things going on in the mind here:

- You don't want your partner but are frightened that somebody else will.
- You're not happy in the relationship but you might be unhappier out if it.
- Everybody else thinks your partner is wonderful.
- You don't want to be on your own and you might not find anybody else.
- It's not perfect but better the devil you know...
- You don't love them any more but you might regret it if you leave.

Well, not one single one of those concepts is a valid reason to stay with somebody you no longer want to be with, no matter how wonderful you believe them to be. They could be the most desired person on the face of the planet but if they just don't 'hit the spot' for you, then as far as you're concerned they are *not* the most desired person on the face of the planet. But somebody else might be and it wouldn't matter if everybody else thought they were weird, ugly or anything else, they would still be the one for you. So the easiest answer for this situation is to forget all about the 'wrong thing' or the 'right thing' and just decide what you *actually want*. And if you're 'hovering', it's odds on that what you want is out.

Sometimes, people are afraid to leave a relationship in case they later see their partner looking ecstatically happy with somebody else. This is a totally natural reaction, since it will irritate you that they just weren't like that with you. All that means, though, is that the relationship just wasn't working, however much you wanted it to. It's always a joint effort and if it's not working properly for one of you, it's not working properly for either of you. After all, there's absolutely no point in being with somebody who would prefer to be with somebody else, since they simply don't have what it takes to make you properly happy. (Commitment to you, in case you're wondering...)

Here's a question that might help you decide what to do (it's been talked about before in this book, so it might seem familiar): *If you knew beyond doubt that within a month of leaving this one, you would be with somebody that set your heart and loins on fire, what would you do?*

For most people, that would be what is known widely today as a 'no brainer'. And all you can guarantee is that if you stay with the one you're with, you probably *won't* meet the one who lights the blue touch paper...

The other end of things

Of course, it might well be the case that none of the foregoing is relevant to you at all because you're not trying to get out of a relationship at all. Instead, you might be in that peculiar kind of 'twilight world' where things really aren't going that well between you and your partner but you're still together. Or perhaps you know things aren't right, but you're just hanging on in there in the hope that, somehow or other, things will right themselves. It's even possible that although there's nothing you can put your finger on, you just have some sort of niggling doubt that all is not well.

If, until now, you've considered your relationship to be absolutely sound and you're only reading this out of interest, don't let what you've read so far convince you there's something you're just not being told about!

There are several doubts that can play on your mind when you have that uneasy feeling that your partner is losing interest:

- There might be somebody else in the background.
- You might just be imagining there's something wrong.
- If you rock the boat you might *make* something go wrong.
- It's just your imagination – you're being neurotic, needy or anxious.

These thoughts, and others like them, serve one very specific purpose – they stop you from having to confront the issue with your partner. But this situation is like an illness, in the sense that the longer you leave it without treatment, the worse it's likely to get. It really doesn't matter if it *is* 'all in your mind' – even if that's the case, it's all in your mind for a reason. If the relationship was sound *and right for you,* you wouldn't be likely to have those feelings of uncertainty. Actually, there is an exception here and that's where this sort of thing happens to you in every relationship you are in, in which case it might be that you have a problem with self-esteem. That's not covered in great detail in this book but there are many places you can find help for such a situation, some listed in the **Resources** section at the end.

For a moment or two, let's just suppose you're right and your partner really would prefer not to be with you any more – the situation is important, the reasons for it are not. It *is* entirely possible that addressing this will bring it to a head and might well be the end of the relationship once and for all. But do you really want to be with somebody who doesn't want to be with you? How will you find the joy that comes from knowing that you're loved and supported and that you are never actually on your own in the world? Even if things seem to improve for a little while, it's likely to be only a matter of time before you're back in the same boat, and all the time this is going on you're missing the chance of discovering the person who will love you as much as you love them.

Without doubt, the best course of action is to take charge of the situation. This is an **active state** rather than a **reactive state.** Active states, where you're actually doing something, are far more productive than reactive states, where you just sit and worry about what's happening or might be happening later. If there's nothing wrong, your partner will soon reassure you and all will be well. If you're right, however, you deserve to find that out for yourself, rather than wait to be told it's over.

Remember, your feelings are your feelings. You didn't choose them and there has to be a reason for them, even if it turns out to be due to a misunderstanding of some sort or some other perfectly valid reason. There's only one way to find out and that is to talk to your partner. Starting such a conversation is never easy and it *will* create some discomfort all round... though that must not deter you. To help, here are a few ways to get the conversation started:

- *"I need to ask you about something. Is that ok?"*
- *"I'm a bit twitchy about something – can I talk to you about it?"*
- *"When you've got a minute, there's something I want to talk about."*
- *"It might be just me but I'm not sure we're all right. Are we?"*
- *"I've been worrying myself sick about something..."*
- *"Somehow, I've got it into my head that there's something wrong between us."*

- *"Are you okay? I feel as if there's something wrong."*

Whatever the direction of the conversation after the opening you choose, be sure to begin it by talking about how you feel, not about what your partner has been doing that has led you to feel like that. It's not so much what your partner says in reply that's important here but the *way* it's said, and if they don't make the effort to be totally reassuring, it's pretty certain that you were right all along. Then it's up to you to decide what to do... And remember an Active state is far better than a Reactive state. Take charge, and you'll feel a lot better than if you just wait for the inevitable, harbouring a faint hope that it never comes.

*Your partner's reaction when you tell them they are about to become your **ex** partner will either turn things round completely or allow you to leave with your head held high.*

Either way, you can look forward to a better future.

Chapter Twelve

Putting it all back together again

It's not completely unknown for a couple to get back together after having separated. The trouble is, it's also not completely unknown for the relationship to fail for a second time. The reason is quite simple – nothing has changed and if you keep on doing what you've always done, you'll keep on getting what you always got!

Before we look at the ins and outs of giving a second go a good working chance, it's worth knowing that the length and type of separation has quite a bearing on the likelihood of success. Consider the following situations, where we assume in each case that both partners are single once more and considering trying again:

1 The break was brief and they remained in touch, mostly amicably, on an almost daily basis.
2 They split up, each found a new partner, and saw nothing of each other for several years.
3 The break was full of animosity until they simply ceased contact.
4 After the break, one found a new partner but the other remained single, though was in frequent touch with their 'Ex' and their new partner.
5 They split up, each found a new partner, but kept amicably in touch.
6 After the break, one found a new partner but the other remained single. They lost touch for a long time.

Of those six scenarios, the first two have the best chance of working comfortably the second time round, though for quite different reasons. In the first one, there is a wish, albeit maybe subconscious, to get back together or perhaps to have never separated in the first place. This is evidenced by the fact that they are still in touch, are amicable, and the break has not had the chance to 'set' and become a habituation. As long as they *truly want* to get back together and as long as the reasons for the split have been resolved, they have a better-than-evens chance of restarting and making it work.

In the second instance, they are 'even', in that they both found new partners, and the passage of time and life experience means that they might now be a better match for each other than they were before. But this scenario is entirely different from the first; they will need to spend time together on a dating basis to see how they 'work' together. They need to explore the problems that caused the break-up – especially if they were sexual – to see how they feel about those things now. Also, they will each need to recognise that the other is a different person from who they were. And if *either* of them is not, the chances of success are greatly diminished.

Numbers 3 and 4 scenarios are fraught with risk! In number 3, the animosity is likely to flare again, since it was never resolved in the first place, simply abandoned. It could still be smouldering, just waiting for something to stoke it up. Number 4 is unequal; one had a new partner, the other one could only observe that new partnership and remained single. There is a strong possibility of comparisons being made here by both, along with defensive postures and maybe even recriminative behaviour from either one about all manner of issues – what was the sex like, why did they keep hanging around, why was it flaunted in their face, no wonder it didn't last... The spiteful or jealous mind can be very inventive!

As for numbers 5 and 6, well there is not as much chance as with 1 and 2 but considerably more than 3 and 4. It depends on which way the wind blows...

Getting it on for the second time...

The reason for the break up in the first place is important of course – if it has not been resolved or in some way rendered inactive, then there's still going to be trouble at some point. Some wounds don't or won't heal, especially if one partner subconsciously doesn't actually want them to. That's not as rare as you might think, either, because resentment can simmer just below the surface, the owner of it just biding their time until there's an opportunity to get their own back. They are not necessarily aware of the situation, since it can be an entirely subconscious process. A clumsy example is: *The person who has been dumped who does everything they can to get back with their partner. They make promises, buy gifts, are attentive, affectionate... And just when things begin to look as if they're fully on track – they get fed up and dump the one who dumped them!* From the outside, it looks like a deliberate act of revenge; from the inside, it can feel as if they gave it their best shot but suddenly realised that they were having to make just too much effort to keep someone they weren't even sure they wanted any more.

There's a lot to 'take on board' about getting a relationship to work properly the second time around, but before we investigate all that, we're going to have a look at two of the major reasons why a break up might happen in the first place. There are many others of course, but after what is classified as 'mutual incompatibility' in divorce courts, these are responsible between them for the majority of splits.

- Abusive behaviour.
- Infidelity.

Sometimes the two are linked and it could be said that the second, infidelity, is actually a form of abuse anyway, especially if it's a repeated circumstance. Here though, they're treated as separate issues, because that way you'll be able to see that even after the massive hurt they create, there is still a faint chance of getting things working properly again. In fact, as daft as it sounds, things might work better the second time around precisely *because* of the huge hurt that was created.

In order for this to be the case, something has to change deep in the mind of the person who was committing the abuse or infidelity. It can't be manufactured in the normal way (though a good therapist might manage it) and has to come about as a moment of intense realisation and equally intense discomfort. If it's profound enough, it will 'stick' and all that is necessary then is for the other partner to recognise the change and be prepared to take the risk of getting back together. The change that's needed in the subconscious is the same in both cases – abuse or infidelity – and is based on shock. It can be summed up in a simple internal thought: *"I did this!"*

Now, just the thought on its own is not sufficient to create the change – there has to also be a profound emotional response, and this is why it cannot happen while the couple are still an item (as mentioned in the last chapter.) It's not produced by just a single recognition or understanding – several things must all happen literally within a nano-second, far faster than conscious thought, when they combine to create a sense of personal devastation:

- A sudden recognition they're not 'getting away with it.'
- A sudden recognition of how much they want to be with their partner.
- A realisation that their partner is definitely not coming back.
- A surge of hurt that strikes at their very core.
- A realisation that they are solely responsible for the problem.

Physical collapse is not unusual when this happens, even with the normally defiant **Warrior** personality, though it is more likely with the highly demonstrative **Nomad.** The Warrior is more likely to have been abusive either physically or emotionally, while the Nomad is more likely to have been unfaithful and in both cases, their normally selfish thought processes have been overridden by a recognition of devastating loss – probably at least equal to the pain they've caused.

This is not to say that all Warriors are likely to be abusers or all Nomads are likely to be philanderers! They're not, of course. But the personality profile of abusers and philanderers can still be defined and they're not likely to be Settlers.

In the moment that that cascade of events occurs, it is as if some instinctive process in their 'core values' makes a shift. They've experienced intense pain that they don't ever want to feel again... and their subconscious begins to work in a subtly different way. It might *look* as if they have discovered a new respect for their partner but in reality they are looking after self, subconsciously seeking to avoid a rerun of those devastating emotions that they glimpsed so briefly. That doesn't matter though, because it's the recognition of how much they want their partner that's caused it and their subconscious processes will filter out any temptation to return to their old ways, or at least, combine such temptation with a strong aversive reaction.

The essential process that must happen here is quite simple – somehow, the individual must 'hit the deck' and realise they've caused catastrophic damage to their relationship. The sad thing about this process is that it usually only occurs after their partner has left and has already managed to dissociate themselves so completely, that any thoughts of returning to the relationship are a matter of complete indifference. They are 'over it' and it's unlikely that there would be any point in trying to rekindle anything. On the rare occasions where there *is* a second chance though, which is usually in situation 1 of the break up scenarios at the beginning of this chapter, it can be better, stronger and more loving the second time around, as long as the 'wronged' partner is able to perform a specific emotional task. And that's what we're going to look at next.

Acceptance

There are many people who will tell you that in order to reestablish a relationship with somebody who has wronged you, it is necessary to forgive them and what they did. The problem with that is that it is enormously difficult, if not downright impossible, for a lot of people to understand exactly how to do that. Those that promote the idea insist that it doesn't mean you are letting anybody get away with anything, more that you're setting yourself free from pain. Somehow, that works for a few people, though it's entirely possible that they are simply dissociating themselves from the pain, which many individuals are just not able to do. To them, the notion of 'forgiving' *feels* like letting somebody off and it usually goes very much against the grain to do that when you've been hurt. It certainly won't repair anything.

Fortunately, there's a more easily understandable, more accessible process that also sets you free from pain and that is the condition of *acceptance*. There's no doubt at all that lack of acceptance causes pain, and pain would be a very unhealthy thing to be harbouring while trying to rebuild your relationship. But it really doesn't have to be that way as long as you can fully understand what acceptance actually is. This next paragraph (in italics) will help you to do just that:

*When something has happened, it cannot be **unhappened**. If it caused pain or distress, it can and will continue to do so until we accept the fact that it is now a part of our life, just as is the problem that was the cause of it. That problem is now in the past and cannot be altered, no matter what we do. Our life will be different from what it was before but no matter how much we hate that fact, how much we want to get back to the way things were, all the anger, resentment and frustration in the world will not make it better – only worse. We can grossly upset our body chemistry, our emotional stability, maybe even create damage*

in other areas; but the only effect is that we feel even more wretched...
and what happened has still happened. Nothing has changed for the
better. Recognise this fact, work to accept the situation as a valid and
irrevocable part of our journey through life, accommodate it into our
psyche, and we will be the best we can under the new circumstances.

If you are in a situation where this is important, you might
now be indignant at the idea of just accepting it and letting it go.
If so, read that paragraph again and recognise that it is all about
helping *you*, rather then helping somebody to get away with
something they did. And if you just are not able to get your head
round the idea, where you are hot-bloodedly resisting even the
very notion, then it's important that you dismiss any idea of
restarting the relationship with the person who was the cause of
what you feel.

On the other hand, if it resonated with you and made sense,
you are probably now experiencing a sensation of calm, and
already beginning to let go of any residual resentment and blame
that might still be lurking somewhere in the shadows of your
mind. Only when they are completely banished – because a
relationship and the failure of it is a joint effort – will you have
the opportunity to find true contentment. When this all makes
complete sense to you, use the process whenever it's necessary.
Teach it to others who need it, too, because this will strengthen it
in your own mind. It's one of the most powerful emotional
healing concepts that exist, and in fact there are many therapists
around the world who use it with their clients to set them free
from pain. It works!

One last thing about acceptance – don't forget to include
yourself! If you believe you contributed in some way to the
problems that have beset you, then you're probably right... But
just accept that fact as well, and resolve to do things as differently as necessary in the future. All the self-recrimination in the
world, all the beating yourself up, pouring scorn upon yourself
and calling yourself a "****dy idiot" won't fix anything.

Acceptance will though.

The rules

"If you don't tell somebody your rules, you can't blame them when they break them!"

That statement was never so true as when you're seeking to mend a broken relationship and restore it to something better than it was in the first place. If there's something that causes you a problem, it's no good keeping quiet on the basis that you're frightened if you talk about it everything will go 'pear shaped' again. If it was part of the problem then it must either be resolved, or you just have to accept that it is 'part of the package' that is this union. What we are saying here, of course, is that you should never go back into something that broke without a lot of discussion and heart-searching to see if change can be sustained – because if it can't, we're back to what you read at the beginning of this chapter: *If you keep on doing what you've always done, you'll keep on getting what you always got!*

If you know you're inclined to be 'picky' – beware! You really cannot expect somebody to be able to make changes to involuntary things like snoring, the way they laugh, the volume of their sneezes, the way they sit on the sofa, and so on. All those things and others like them are just part and parcel of how they are, and you can't justifiably make a whole bunch of rules about them. In general, though, those are not the things that need discussion. It's 'stuff' like dismissing feelings, public ridicule, spiteful teasing, unnecessary criticism, rash spending, not helping around the house... Just about anything that rankles and is under conscious control.

Now, because many – maybe all – those things are frequently part of habituation, expect to have to give a **calm** reminder from time to time; and if it's you that's being reminded, accept the reminder with an apology. In even the longest established relationships, there's no reason for a lack of politeness and respect – in fact, such a lack can be the cause of problems in the first place.

Getting sex back on track

Without doubt, this can be the biggest hurdle of all, especially if the break up was as a result of infidelity. There is sometimes an oddity here, too, in that the person who had the affair might experience the most difficulty in getting back to normality. As a result, their partner might perceive that any unwillingness is an indicator of a continued hankering for the individual with whom they cheated... and, of course, it might be, especially for a while. When somebody has been unfaithful but are reconciled with their original partner, the following circumstances are common for them during sexual activity:

- Males are unable to get or maintain an erection.
- Females fail to lubricate and experience discomfort as a result.
- Males sometimes cannot ejaculate.
- Females frequently cannot achieve orgasm.
- They feel as if they are being unfaithful *now,* but to their lover.
- They discover they are unable to get their lover out of their mind.
- They feel their partner is only doing it because they feel they should.

They will probably not want to talk about any of this, for obvious reasons, and it's by no means certain that such a discussion would achieve anything worthwhile at all. The reverse might well be the case, in fact. So if you're in this situation where your partner strayed and you observe or suspect one or more of those 'symptoms', you can either just wait for time to do the healing – and it probably will – or you can take an active part in fixing things more quickly. What you need to provide is easily summed up in one word: **Affection.**

Now, if you are recoiling from the very idea of being affectionate to the person who cheated on you and caused you pain, remember:

- You wanted them back so presumably you love them still.
- Resentment will achieve nothing except more pain for both of you.
- If they are happier *you* will be happier.
- It is *your* relationship as well as theirs.
- Punishment and/or gloating will eventually finish this 'restart'.
- It was as difficult for them to come back as it was for you to accept them.
- They are hurting and they are with *you*.

So bearing the above in mind, help them to feel that they are with the one they really want to be with and recovery will be much speedier. Nobody said it was going to be easy, and there's certainly a lot more to it than is covered in this chapter – but this book has most, if not all, of what you need. If you really want it to work, then you have to give it your best shot. There's absolutely no point in even trying if you're expecting your partner to be full of contrition and therefore make all the effort. It went wrong for both of you and it will take both of you to get it right.

Chapter Thirteen

What's love got to do with it?

This chapter is all about surviving and enjoying a long-term relationship – not just coping with it or somehow managing to put up with seeing the same face every breakfast time, but actually being pleased you're there. If you already are, it would be a bit of a surprise that you're reading this book... so it's likely that you're looking to your future. Well, you're in the right place.

If you ask almost any couple who've been together a long time if they still love each other, they will be likely to answer: *"Well, yes, of course!"* or similar. If you then ask them if they are still *in love* with each other, the answer is likely to be more hesitant. The truth is, many people aren't really sure they understand the distinction between loving somebody and being *in love* with them. It's a romantic notion and maybe nothing more than that, though some feel that you can love somebody in the way you would a parent or a sibling or close friend, but you would only be *in love* with a romantic partner. Even that doesn't really work, though, because the type of love you feel for somebody where sex would never be an option feels quite different to the sort of love where it is. It sometimes gets bandied around as an excuse to end a relationship: *"I love you but I'm not in love with you..."* making others question what this is all about and maybe leaving them wondering if they're missing out in some mysterious way.

So let's get rid of some of the uncertainty and worry, so that you don't have to go around examining your deepest inner thoughts to see if you're 'in love' with somebody. For the moment, forget the sort of love you feel for family and friends and think instead about the stuff that surges all over the place and creates joy, anxiety, exhilaration, worry, fear, jealousy, uncertainty, obsessive texting, emails in the early hours... and the inability to concentrate on very much else. In the beginning of such a relationship, you would travel four hours there and back to spend just thirty minutes with the object of your affection... yet when the excitement settles down (as it always does) you might not drive thirty minutes there and back to spend four hours with them. All totally normal.

If you've never experienced such a breath-taking emotional roller-coaster as new love then you're in for a shock when it does happen.

There's no mystery about the 'magic ingredient' – it's sex! When somebody is physically attractive to you and their body scent 'hits the spot' (which you usually won't consciously notice), it's likely that your DNA is sufficiently different to make breeding a good prospect. Of course, we are not able to interpret it like that; to us, it just feels as if we're totally 'smitten', which is why it's so powerful. The DNA 'thing' is why we don't usually find our siblings sexually attractive. Their DNA is so similar to ours that their body scent acts as a deterrent for sexual arousal, to avoid undesirable interbreeding. All of this is buried deep in the subconscious, of course, an integrated part of the 'human condition' of which we have no conscious awareness. There are a few problems associated with this physical and rather 'animalistic' response pattern to desirable individuals and most of us become familiar with them at some point in our life:

- A sudden and ferocious mutual attraction with an 'inappropriate' somebody.
- The attraction to somebody who doesn't feel the same way.
- The attentions of somebody to whom we are not attracted at all.

Of those three, the first is the most dangerous and can easily create an irresistible energy that wrecks relationships. It can generate deeply painful feelings of regret about what never was or can never be. It changes the life of an individual like nothing else ever could – and not usually for the better. It *feels* like love and physically interferes with the workings of our brain chemistry, just as it is designed to do... Because **nature** knows nothing of morals, marriages, promises and vows. Nature knows about one thing in particular and that is *how to make certain the species keeps going.*

Just a fleeting thing

So what does this have to do with surviving in, and enjoying, a long-term relationship? A lot, actually! Sexual attraction is fleeting, nothing more than body chemistry that brings people together in the first place. It will fade after a few months, maybe a couple of years, and it's then that somebody might leave for pastures new, with that phrase: *"I love you but I'm not in love with you..."* By now, you probably understand that what that really means is: *"I don't want to have sex with you any more..."* The relationship was a physical one but had little or no emotional connection. Not only that but the departing individual is once again in search of that heady, addictive, chemistry that comes at the beginning of a new relationship (which they might already have found, of course.)

On the other hand, when there *are* emotional ties, when the couple *like* each other and feel as if they are friends, there can still be joy in the union long after the passion has subsided to weekly events. Or fewer. If there are children, that circumstance can hold them together for a while but doesn't necessarily contribute to a happy co-existence – and anyway, we're really talking here about the couple themselves. Their relationship shares more than body fluids. They like the same things, want to do things together, and each one values the other. They are therefore far more likely to resist any of those 'inappropriate' attractions without regret than they otherwise would be – *and it's a fact that almost everybody gets at least one of those temptations at some point.*

This bonding process doesn't happen by accident. It's not even truly 'normal' for the human animal, because we don't have any form of 'pair-bonding' gene in our biological make-up. Except during sexual intercourse, that is, when we get that flood of 'oxytocin' into our system that creates wonderful feelings of love and closeness… well, as long as we're not concentrating solely on self anyway. So if from the beginning you enjoyed your partner's company, irrespective of sexuality, and they yours, then you have a much better chance of sustaining that relationship for a lifetime. But it's still only a chance, because it needs a little more – it needs *awareness* of certain aspects of life and living together. It needs some *effort* by both of you to get the best out of it.

Personality comes into it, and we've already looked at what constitutes a good match or otherwise. Keeping sexual interest alive and well is desirable and we've had a look at that, too. We've even considered how to handle the inevitable disagreements. All those things come into it but they are mostly about simple survival, where what we are looking at here is about *enjoying* that survival.

Friends

It's not a surprise that some of the happiest relationships are between people who knew each other almost or totally platonically for some time before they became a couple. They knew each other as friends, insulated from the disappointments that exist solely within a close relationship, like when sex goes wrong for instance, or when there are money worries, illness, disagreements and all the other 'stuff' of marriage – whether or not that marriage is official. They have created a habituation of friendliness and regard which has become normal for them… So that when, for whatever reasons, they become an 'item' instead of just two individuals who like each other, they already have a framework on which their closer coupling can rest.

So from the very beginning, search to truly understand what

makes your partner 'tick'. Set out from the start to make them your friend and not your rival – and be sure that you are not setting yourself up as *their* rival either. Learn the things they like and see if you like them too... And tell them about the things you like, no matter whether that's about food, drink, films, furniture or sex. Especially sex – your partner deserves to know what you like in that department just as you do in theirs. There's no room for coyness or delicacy when it comes to *that* particular behaviour. As mentioned before, the last thing good sex is, is delicate or coy!

Any relationship can be enjoyed for life, though personality comes into it to a large extent. You've already read about some of that but here's a bit more that might be useful to understand:

- The **Warrior** will seldom make it obvious that they're happy in a relationship, though this doesn't mean they're not. They will usually address directly any issue they're not happy about. If that's the way you are, tread gently!
- The **Settler** may want more from the relationship than they feel able to say, though they will respond to some fairly gentle questioning if necessary. If you're a Settler, take a deep breath and *say something*.
- The **Nomad** is happy when they're the centre of attention, though will adore making others feel good if they are being rewarded with praise. If that's you, think how best to often please your partner so they think you're amazing!

It can come as a surprise to some that most good relationships are not quite as evenly balanced as most might believe. It's often a close-run thing but more often than not, one half of the couple turns out to be a little more of a 'giver' and the other a little more of a 'taker'. As long as both are happy in their role – and because they are both working with their natural instinctive behaviour pattern they usually are – this is all part of the easy stability that makes the whole thing work so well. If you're the giver, which is highly likely since you're the one reading this book, it might sometimes seem that it's always you looking after the relationship... but perhaps that's just because you're better at it than your partner! Of course, you can always leave the book lying open at the page you want them to read, or even talk about it directly, as long as you don't sound accusing in your manner (or as if you're trying to become a taker.)

Now we're going to have a look at four specific and often intertwined situations that can prevent a relationship entering or sustaining long-term harmony. It forms a kind of 'list of avoids' to help give you the best chance of growing old happily with the same partner.

Boredom

This is probably the easiest of habituations to fall into – it's an almost natural response to stability and familiarity, and can be hugely damaging to a relationship if it's allowed to become obvious. For instance, rolling your eyes and saying: *"What now?"* in a bored tone of voice when your partner starts to talk to you is hardly encouraging for continued conversation. There are actually a couple of 'Golden Rules' about boredom. The first is that your partner shouldn't see it, and the second is that you shouldn't expect them to sort it out. It's *your* boredom, stemming from *your* approach to life and living, and only you can truly find the answer.

There's something very important to think about here, too. If you frequently find yourself feeling bored, try to find out why and discover a way to fix the problem, even if you come to the realisation that it's your relationship that's at the bottom of it. Similarly, if you notice that your partner seems bored, seek to get them talking about it because if could be to your benefit as well as theirs. Boredom is a destructive and highly contagious force (others around you can easily catch it!) and needs to be addressed as early as possible, so that if it's coming from within the relationship there's a chance to sort it out before too much damage is done. It's worth noting, too, that *sounding* bored is the best way to continue *being* bored. It's an interesting thing that 'doing' cheerful can lead to you actually *feeling* cheerful. If you doubt that, try this exercise: *stand up and make a shape as if something wonderful has just happened, big smile, arms in the air perhaps, eyes shining with excitement. While you're holding that pose, say 'I feel really, really bored today' and make it sound as if you mean it, but without changing the 'excited' face and shape.* This is just about impossible and the exercise shows you how closely associated your mind and body are, no matter how much you might want to believe they are separate.

Auto-contrariness

This is usually an indicator of the individual who has begun to subconsciously see their partner as a rival and one who must be kept in check, at that. More often than not, it's the combination of Warrior and Nomad personality types, and the Warrior has gradually assumed the role, without knowing it, of a 'brake'. This sometimes has its roots in unacknowledged or unrecognised jealousy of the personable manner and enthusiasm of the Nomadic mind. It's also based on the Warrior tendency to see what is *not* while the Nomad instinctively looks for what *is* – and so often seems to find it. Even when the Warrior partner enjoys the liveliness that the Nomad injects into the relationship, that tendency to pessimism can still make itself felt. It manifests in many ways but this snippet of an imaginary conversation will give you the idea:

Nomad: *"Hey, there's a fantastic new restaurant opened in the High Street! Shall we give it a try tonight?"*

Warrior: *"I don't really think that's a good idea. I mean, everything's new and they might not have got the menu right yet."*

Nomad: *"Oh, come on! If we don't like it much, we can always* *leave."*

Warrior: *"Almost certainly a waste of time, anyway. It'll probably be crowded with no tables free."*

Nomad: *"That's not a problem – I'll phone and make a reservation."*

Warrior: *"Oh, ok, if you must. But don't blame me if it's awful."*

You can see the Warrior determinedly trying to keep control of the situation, even preparing for an 'I told you so' situation if things aren't good. Now, just for fun, see if you can imagine how the conversation might have gone with another Nomad, or with a Settler. You can probably have a good go at getting it right now, but there are no prizes for that!

Although the Warrior and Nomad can be an excellent combination, if you're the Warrior it's important to value and respect that Nomad enthusiasm – it's part of the lifeblood of your relationship even if you don't realise it, and it shouldn't be crushed. And if you're the Nomad, it's equally important to remember that the Warrior is a bit of a pessimist by nature and is only trying to keep things on an even and balanced keel. It's what they do. Let them do it, if only now and again.

Criticism

Criticism is another killer as far as harmony is concerned – and there's a lot to be said for that old adage: 'All criticism is self-criticism'. Some people might scoff at that, but it's a form of attack when we criticise another, and we only really attack that which we fear or despise. There are two main triggers:

- Noticing something about the other person that reminds us of something we don't like very much, maybe even part of ourselves.
- Noticing something in or about the other person that we don't have but feel as if we should, and therefore feel lacking in some way.

We don't always recognise the process – it's one of those things that goes on in the subconscious mind and all we notice is that we don't like something the other person does or *is*. Perhaps they remind us of someone we once knew who hurt us. Maybe they are successful and we feel that we are not, so we rationalise it by asserting that they don't deserve it. Occasionally *jealousy* can trigger the reaction but whatever its root, criticising the other person makes us feel better, as if we are in some way superior. If you're still not too sure about this, there's another odd aspect to consider and that is that there is often an irrational anger associated with the critical remark. It might not be particularly profound, but it's usually there, in some form or another, which is why we want to attack, of course.

The rule doesn't change even when we deliver something we fondly couch in that friendly term: 'constructive criticism'. It's still criticism and the only difference is that the 'criticisee' can make something positive out of it if they wish, which gives the 'criticiser' a nice warm glow of having been right! They can take some credit for the enhancement... which leads us straight back into the process of feeling in some way superior of course.

Whatever the trigger, criticising your partner – especially if it's on a frequent basis – will chip away at even the most loving relationship, so if you find yourself doing this, stop and ask yourself what you're seeking to achieve. Are you really trying to make a positive change or are you just seeking to score points? What is it that you *really* want to happen? And if the criticism achieved that goal, would you be completely happy about everything else? Maybe not – jealousy is often an indicator of some far deeper issue that needs to be sorted out.

If it's you that's on the receiving end (even if your partner criticises you for being critical), never immediately assume that it's justified. Instead examine the situation as honestly as you can, keeping any retaliatory response under control while you do so. If it eventually seems to you that your partner is right, then say so and apologise. But watch out for something else to become the focus of that critical attention and if you find it, start examining the entire relationship more closely, because there might be something that needs urgent attention.

On rare occasions, there is no pleasure being taken in the act of criticising and the only reason for its delivery is an honest recognition of the scope for some sort of improvement. But then, it's not so much a criticism as an observation and it can easily form a valuable part of a loving relationship as long as both halves of the couple are at ease with it.

We'll finish this section with an example of the same remark being delivered first as a criticism and secondly as an observation. Imagine one half of the couple rearranging the furniture in a room; the other realises that the sofa is partly blocking the radiator:

"What on earth have you put the sofa in front of the radiator for? It'll make the room freezing cold in the winter!"

"Hmm... Looks nice. I'm wondering if the sofa might soak up the heat from the radiator though."

Hopefully, you won't have to wonder which is the best approach!

Sex and sexuality

This is potentially one of the thorniest of areas in a relationship and, of course, we've looked at some of the elements of it before in the book, especially **Chapter Six** – *Sex and Sexuality*. But a chapter about harmony in a long-established union wouldn't be complete without including a section on sex. Without doubt, the biggest difficulty is the differing levels of drive between males and females. Within an established relationship, it is not unusual for the female to steadily become less immediately interested than the male. This has nothing to do with loving him less, and everything to do with her evolutionary history – females never did have to think about or search for sex because it has always come to them. When her partner passes near her, she might smile but it may have more to do with companionship and familiarity than sex. She loves him still but is in the 'buffer zone', that part of the female thought processes associated with day-to-day living and separated from sexual arousal.

He, on the other hand, if he still loves her, will look at her bottom almost every time she walks anywhere near him; he will also look, in no particular order, at her neck, hair, ears, shoulders, breasts, waist, ankles and probably everything else. And he will think of sex. *This does* **NOT** *mean that she has become just a sexual object, a 'vagina on legs'.* He has no choice in the matter, in the same way that she has no choice about the 'buffer zone'. Neither state is decided upon – they are both totally natural and automatic facets of being.

The 'buffer zone' is incomprehensible to the male. He doesn't have one and most don't even realise what it is or that it exists. The male 'instant readiness' can be a source of irritation for the female. She might not recognise that if he desires her, he desires her all the time. He can't switch it off, though he will keep it under some form of control, which really only means not going on about it all the time!

Remember, we cannot control our feelings, only what we do with them – you've heard that a few times now! As it happens though, in a good relationship there's often an unspoken and tacitly accepted compromise situation that can work well for most couples. The compromise is that he won't keep on and on about it if she does it and seems to enjoy it reasonably frequently. And she'll do it reasonably frequently, appearing to enjoy it, as long as he doesn't make too much of a song and dance about it on the occasions when she really isn't very keen.

This may never be spoken about, the couple finding their way into this comfortable 'working relationship' by the passage of time and experience. They might have sex three times a week or four times a year, and provided neither of them is harbouring resentment about it, all will be well. Sexual intercourse might be violently passionate or gentle and loving and, again, if neither of them secretly yearns for something different, all is well.

Now think about the other three concepts we've been looking at in this chapter: **Boredom, Auto-contrariness** and **Criticism**... It's when any of those find their way into the sex life of a couple that the problems really begin. *Chapter Sixteen contains further information to help improve the sexual side of a relationship.*

Chapter Fourteen

A trick or two to deal with a break up

This Chapter will show you how surviving a break up needn't be as devastating as it usually seems, especially when you employ the self-help method shown later. We'll start, though, with another look at the notion of acceptance – only here, it has a slightly different 'slant'.

The break-up of a relationship, especially a long-standing one, is one of the most painful situations that the human psyche can experience. We are bereaved just as surely as if the other person had died – in fact, the pain can be *worse* than if death had occurred (we look at the physical death of a partner in another chapter) because the knowledge that an 'Ex' is still somewhere around, possibly laughing and loving with somebody else, can generate emotionally devastating pain and resentment. The grief might not actually be for what has actually been lost, but for what the relationship never was, and that can make it all the more difficult to bear. Somebody might soldier on for months – years, even – in the belief that they *are* loved and wanted, only to be unceremoniously dumped for a replacement. Then, the longing to wind the clock back in order to exact some sort of punishment or revenge, or do something different, can become all but unbearable. Suicidal thoughts are not uncommon in these circumstances.

But it doesn't have to be that way.

Acceptance behaves like a magical balm, allowing the individual to move on, to make new plans, to find new happiness and new fun. When it is fully accepted at a subconscious level that the person who has left is not coming back, all the longing, begging and waiting can stop. There is no longer any need to keep on listening for the telephone to ring or to anxiously scan every email, text, or piece of mail. When this sort of acceptance happens suddenly, it is almost as if a miracle had occurred. We can smile again and mean it. Unfortunately, there are no magical words that will *make* acceptance happen; it has to come from a deep recognition that just desperately wanting somebody to come back won't make them come back; and anyway, if we somehow manage to find a way to persuade, cajole, force or blackmail a lost lover/companion into returning, what then? We have to be constantly on our guard in case they decide to leave again, because we *know* that they don't truly want to be with us. There's no joy there, only more pain as we are constantly reminded that the relationship is not what we wanted it to be. It's much better to accept, let go, and move forward.

A question...

Here's an interesting question to ponder: *is divorce (and the break up of a long term relationship is emotionally the same thing) the end or the beginning?* It's actually easy to see it as either, and the self-help method later in this chapter will show you how to view it as definitely the beginning. The beginning of a new life, the beginning of a chance to find what you didn't have the last time round – and if you're in this situation right now, just accept that you *didn't* have what you thought you had, no matter how strongly you feel that you did. Whatever the cause of the split was, you wanted to be wanted indefinitely. It didn't happen and you deserve better.

Getting over a break up, especially of a marriage or long-standing relationship, is different for males and females. Females have always had a *sisterhood* dating back to the hunter-gatherer's camps, when the males were out hunting or fighting and the women looked after the young and the old. They would have talked together a lot and the ancient instincts for chatting and commiserating with each other are still present in the psyche. When a female breaks up with her partner, she is allowed to cry.

Her friends support her, cry with her, stroke her and generally look after her, usually reassuring her that she's 'better off without him if he can do that to you'. Women can hug each other, kiss each other, and touch each other without embarrassment or suspicion that there is any intention other than providing comfort. It satisfies that ancient female instinct to nurture, and the recipient will experience a flood of oxytocin that in this case creates a feeling of closeness and companionship to offset the pain.

But what of the male? When a male breaks up with his partner he is not allowed to cry – in public anyway, though many do so in private. He doesn't have a brotherhood that corresponds with the female's sisterhood. When males were out hunting or fighting, there wasn't time for chatter and commiseration. Each one of them was part of a fighting and hunting machine with his particular task to perform, and he needed to 'shelve', suppress, or otherwise thrust aside any personal pain. If he didn't, it could result in death for him or some of the others in his band and the possibility of death certainly focusses the attention! So the instincts the male has inherited are different, geared towards letting go and moving on – though, in truth, most modern males don't do it that well.

His friends' support is likely to involve taking him to the pub and getting him thoroughly drunk, amid laughter (which is often forced) and assurances that there are plenty more fish in the sea. Because the atmosphere is falsely jocular (males often use laughter as a defence against more profound emotional responses) someone is likely to say: *"Yeah, but who wants to go out with a fish?"* to which another might reply: *"Mind you, give it a couple of weeks..."*

Camaraderie, yes. Genuine comfort... Not a lot.

Time distortion

For both males and females after a break up, time plays tricks, especially if they were the one who was 'let go'. The passage of a few minutes feels like an hour and a very long hour at that. Mornings seem to last all day and days seem never-ending... But most of that is because of the hope that the phone will ring, a text will come in or an email will arrive with the message that it's all been a terrible mistake and every effort should be made to restore things to the way they were. That hope is almost never fulfilled and serves only to sustain the pain while you wait. And *all the time you wait.* It's a situation which can go on for months with some people... and what if that call, text or email *does* come? Will you be happy? Or will you wonder if it's going to be any different this time? It usually isn't.

There's an old saying: *"The best way to get over somebody is to get under somebody..."* Yes, it's slightly crude and aimed mostly at females, but it carries a great truth. Of course, it's not usually possible to just go out and strike up a relationship with a new sex partner and most people don't want to, anyway. But that's not the point. The point is that sooner or later you *will* be in a new relationship and the pain of the last one will then become a thing of the past. So what we are really saying here is, as difficult as it can be, let go of that hope that you can be hurt twice by the same person (because that's what it amounts to, most of the time) and concentrate on what you might do differently in your next relationship.

Focus on the future, on the sort of person you might like to be with, and let the past drift further back behind you where it belongs.

Self-help

Now we're going to have a look at what is probably one of the most powerful self-help methods you will ever discover. It's not just for getting you to view the break up situation as an exciting beginning rather than an end, but for anything where you need to make a rapid change to the way you feel about any situation in your life and find a positive attitude that will help you resolve it.

The relationship issue is covered first, but there are a few pointers as to how you could use it in other ways. It's a powerful way of working which was developed by the author of this book in 2000 and is now in use by therapists all over the world. It's actually a modern and dynamic form of an older style of therapy called 'Parts work', 'Parts' referring to different aspects of personality.

It works with the concept that you're already familiar with, the **Warrior, Settler** and **Nomad** personality types, though here, we're going to be looking at how you can use each of those resources *within yourself* to help you look forward to the future with optimism. There's only one catch – you have to allow it to happen! Some people are so intent on hanging on to the past in case the Ex beckons, or in case they miss a chance to get revenge, that they struggle with any notion of finally severing the ties that are hurting them. If you've understood and taken on board what you've read so far though, that's probably not you.

You've already seen the way that each personality 'works' in relationships; so now here's a look at how they function after things have gone wrong (assuming you to be the 'dumpee' and not the 'dumper'):

- The **Warrior** carries resentment and, often, a wish to get even. Anger alternates with depression and, oddly perhaps, this personality tends to gravitate towards both – they will often 'take pleasure in unpleasure' and are usually unwilling to let go of either until they have exhausted the associated energy. In other words, they'll hold on to the whole thing until they get bored with it. Then, they will often flatly refuse to discuss any of it with anybody.
- The **Settler** will hurt the most out of the three types, internalising everything, usually convinced that it was all their fault and that they don't deserve any different. They can

become clingy, seemingly not able to function unless they are surrounded by their friends. It can often seem as if they are milking the situation to get the most stroking out of it – and they might be, sometimes. When others appear finally to be losing interest, they usually start to get better.

• The **Nomad** will usually profess great pain yet seem to be perfectly cheerful – and this personality can often feel both at once and choose which to experience according to their situation. The Nomad usually has no trouble in soon shrugging their shoulders, dusting themselves down, and getting straight back into life. It's not that they don't have real depth of feelings, more that they know instinctively when to move on to the next adventure.

From the above, you can understand two things immediately: (a) Which personality type is most active within your mind – it might not be the one that you discovered yourself to be in **Chapter Two** since this is an extreme circumstance and that sometimes brings a different part to the fore; and (b) Which personality type is the most likely to suffer least and move on more readily. It's important to note, though, that we all have some of each personality in our psychological make up and the more complicated the scenario, the more we are likely to be aware of this. We can also be aware of the internal argument that goes on between the angry part, the sad and needy part, and the 'for-god's-sake-just-let-it-go' part.

This is the 'standard' behaviour pattern for every 'normal' person under the circumstances and the trick is to get the mind and subconscious focussed on the task at hand – feeling better, letting go, and moving on.

Now, if you are already a Nomad personality you might feel that you've got everything sewn up and there's no need to read the rest of this chapter. Well, it's your choice, of course, but then you'll be missing out on learning something that you will usually do better than most, thanks to your creative imagination.

You are about to discover how you can easily switch between different personality behaviour patterns *at will*. Just think how useful that can be in your life; you can access the Warrior part of you when you need to stand firm, take charge, or make your presence felt; the Settler part can help you with negotiation, problem solving, or getting the best out of others; and the Nomad part will help you enjoy life; be optimistic, and inspire others. The best part about it is that once you've learnt the trick, you won't have to think about it – you'll find yourself automatically dropping into the mode you need for any circumstance.

It can be an exciting thought that by the time you get to the end of this chapter you will be able to access each part of your personality with ease and if you're currently in a break up situation, you will have already started to feel better about yourself and your future. There's a little bit of work to do first, though, and it's a good idea to grab yourself a pen and three sheets of paper before continuing; you're going to develop a **Virtual Persona** for each part and you'll see later on how they're going to help you. When you've finished this task, it'll be a good idea to file these three sheets with the profile that you created in **Chapter Two** – you might need them for reference at some time in the future.

Warrior Persona

Take the first sheet and write 'Warrior' at the top... Now let yourself think of ancient warriors – not a modern character but somebody from at least several hundred years ago. They can be male or female (irrespective of your own gender) and you might imagine a Han Archer, Samurai, Knight in Armour, ancient Viking or Norseman, Attila the Hun, Richard the Lionheart, Roman Centurion, Gladiator or anything else that just seems to you to embody the character of the Warrior. Don't worry about 'good' or 'bad' individuals because this is all about determination, resolve, practicality, assertiveness and the ability to stand firm, rather than moral viewpoint. See the image in your mind's eye as best you can (close your eyes if necessary for this) then write down a description of how they look, sound, smell, move and physically feel. Put each element on a separate line and make it all so vivid in your mind that you eventually begin to feel as if you must once have known somebody like this imaginary person. They can have a name, or they can just be 'Warrior'. Notice what it is about them that shows beyond doubt that they are a warrior and write that down in capital letters.

This next part is very important: Once you have everything written down, imagine how this person would feel inside themselves. Take as long as you need and when you have it, make a note of where you get that feeling in your own body. If you struggle a bit, don't worry; just relax and ask yourself is it in your head, your torso, your arms, legs or maybe as a kind of aura that surrounds you and if that's the case, notice what colour it is. Write it in capital letters next to what you wrote about the 'sign' that this is a Warrior. You'll end up with something like: SWORD, SPINE perhaps, or maybe: CROSSBOW, RED AURA.

It's important that you complete this task before moving onto the next and it's not a problem if you have to do these on separate days... and if you're in 'break up' mode at the moment that might be all you can manage. It's fine. It's also fine if you decide to press on and create the other two personas, BUT you should have a short break first. Get a cup of tea and a biscuit and just daydream idly for a few moments.

Settler Persona

Take your second sheet of paper and write 'Settler' at the top of it. Now continue exactly as for the Warrior, again ensuring that your Virtual Persona is of somebody who might have lived many hundreds of years ago. They might be a Farmer, Farmer's Wife, Dressmaker, Hairdresser, Schoolteacher, Philosopher, Cattle

Drover, even an Angel if that's what comes to mind. The important thing about the Settler is that they are unassuming, community-minded and thoughtful. Now, as before, write everything about them putting each element on a separate line and imagine this persona as vividly as you can. See what it is about them that strongly shows their 'Settlerness' and write it down in capital letters.

Next, the same exercise about what this persona would feel like inside themselves; could it be calm, accepting, loving, forgiving, part of a 'bigger picture' or something else? When you have it, explore to see where you found that feeling in your body as you thought of it – and if it's in your physical body it must be in a different place from where you felt the 'essence' of the Warrior. If it's in an aura around you again, though, that's ok, but it needs to be a different colour if that's also where you felt the Warrior. As before, write it down in capitals next to the other one, so that you have something like: SMILE, HEART or perhaps: BOOK, BLUE AURA. Again, pause for a few minutes before starting on the last one, the Nomad – you might find you're already starting to get images in your mind but to avoid the possibility of contamination with Settler ideas, just take that short break.

Nomad Persona

Well, you already know what to write at the top of the third sheet, of course. The Nomad Persona can be a Wandering Minstrel, Bedouin, Actor, Orator, Soothsayer (real or fake), Snake-oil Salesman, Writer, Gypsy, Magician, Illusionist... or just simply an extremely colourful character who might have lived hundreds of years ago. After writing the description, show in capital letters whatever truly reveals them to be a Nomad. Is their essence optimistic, energetic, enthusiastic, wild or something else? Notice where it 'lives' in your body as you vividly imagine them and write it, as with the other two, in capitals. CRYSTAL BALL, LEGS might be something like your answer, or maybe something more cryptic, such as: WHOLE BODY, DYNAMIC AURA.

Practise, practise...

Now you need just a few minutes of practise to truly activate these Virtual Personas in your mind and this is easy to do. First memorise your three word pairs – just for example we'll say they're:

- SWORD, SPINE
- BOOK, BLUE AURA
- CRYSTAL BALL, LEGS

You might have noticed already how those pairs conjure up at least the *thought* of the Virtual Persons they relate to. Now, once you've memorised your own word pairs, close your eyes and think about each in turn for a minute or so, longer if you want to, since it's not particularly time-specific. While you think of them, let yourself get the *feeling* of the essence of each one in your body. It might only be a faint sensation at first but that's okay, because it will get stronger each time you do it – and this is an exercise you can do for a few minutes every day if you want to get the best out of it. You'll notice that you begin to actually *feel different* as you think of each word pair and that's exactly as it should be. After completing five or six minutes of this eyes-closed work, you will find yourself already becoming familiar with it.

Right, you know what to do – So ***do it now!***

*

*

*

*

Good, you're back... Now there are three different ways you can use this Virtual Persona work. One way is easier and more instant than the other two, and that's the one we'll have a look at first. You might have already 'got' the idea of what to do while you were practicing just now, because it is a bit obvious. Just in case, though:

Method one

This is the best one if you're struggling with the break up situation, though it can be used to help you feel better about any problem where there is an emotional response. Observe how you feel for a moment or two, then think of your word pairs one at a time to bring the feeling and image of the associated Virtual Persona into your mind and body. Keep it there for a minute or two and notice how it changes the way you feel about your situation... Then do the same thing with the other two. Do you prefer the feeling of the no-nonsense and down-to-earth Warrior, the accepting and forgiving Settler, or the optimism and forward-looking Nomad? It's up to you, and you can focus on what feels best for as long as you want to – you will recover far more quickly than if you had just those scattered thoughts that were creating conflict.

Method two

This the one to use when you have to do something that you're not certain how best to tackle – perhaps taking charge of a situation and telling somebody *"it's over,"* or maybe the opposite, when you realise you've made a bit of a mess of things and want to repair any damage before it's too late. While holding the task in your mind, think about each word pair and what they stand for. One of them will give you a more positive feeling than the other two, whether it's the assertiveness of the Warrior, the gently communicative abilities of the Settler, or the Nomad's enthusiasm and persuasive inventiveness.

But that's not sufficient on its own here... Once you've decided, do nothing until just before it's time to perform the task, then find yourself a quiet place to sit with your eyes closed for a couple of minutes, anywhere, as long as you won't be disturbed. Bring the image of the Virtual Persona to mind, seeing or thinking of everything you created. The way they look, sound, feel, move... their very essence and the way they *are*. This will work like a 'mind tuning' exercise and even if it's not your natural personality, you will be able to work with those resources without having to think about it for some considerable time afterwards. It's a bit like the way that conversation tunes your mind to the subject being talked about. You don't have to think what to say most of the time – it's automatic, because your subconscious has been instructed as to the subject it should focus on and it does just that. In this instance, it not a conversational subject but a way of being and you can do that too.

If you're not sure about this, have you ever found yourself feeling angry with people who were not the cause of it, because somebody else had wound you up? Well, this is the same thing, except that you've wound yourself up, so you can trust the process!

Method three

This one is more difficult but works well for all sorts of problems, as long as you can use your imagination. It is especially good when you just don't know what to do about a situation, for instance: should you tell your partner it's finished or wait and see what happens? Should you have yet another conversation about the way you feel or give an ultimatum (they usually backfire)? Maybe write them a letter or ask them to marry you to see what happens if they're put under pressure?

You need to find a quiet place where you won't be disturbed for thirty minutes or so – it might not take that long but then again, it might. This one is an eyes-closed routine so you'll need to memorise the gist of it before trying it and fortunately, it's quite easy to hold in your mind:

Close your eyes and think of your word pairs, 'summoning' the

image of each Virtual Persona as you do so. Imagine they're in the room with you and ask each the simple question: "What shall I do about —
— — —- ?" You probably won't actually **hear** *words but the thought will arrive in your head. There's no need to work hard at this, because you only need to think what this person might say if they were a real person, somebody you know. When you have all three answers you can either choose the one you like best (after all, it is* **your** *idea!) or you can ask them to help you decide between them which is actually the best one. Again, you probably won't hear words but you will get a distinct feeling of what's best.* **Don't question it!** *It comes from the depths of your subconscious mind and that part of you knows everything about you.*

As you can see, that's not too difficult to remember. But it is a good idea to practise a couple of times before asking about anything really serious – you can even ask things like: *"How am I doing in my life?"* just to get used to that rather strange idea of talking to those parts of self! What you've read here is similar to the way a professional therapist would use it and it has already helped thousands of people to find a better life.

Now it's your turn...

Chapter Fifteen

A scary thing happened on the way...

For some people, there is only one problem in a relationship... in *any* relationship, and that is a fear of commitment. Rather unimaginatively called 'Commitmentphobia', this can affect males or females, though most of the time it is a fear, rather than a true phobia – and there is a difference. Very loosely, a phobia is the imagined certainty of dying if having to face the phobic object; a fear, which can be extraordinarily profound, is not associated with dying but of something unknown.

For a long time, most people assumed that this fear of commitment affected only males, anxious about losing their freedom to marriage, but that was probably because the females just kept quiet about it! Also, this was in the days when the main measure of commitment to another was a gold ring and a certificate signed by an official stating that they had been joined together and should not be put asunder. The likelihood is that there are as many females who want to avoid washing somebody's socks and underpants as there are males who don't want their outings with the lads curtailed. There are as many females who want to hang on to a carefree do-as-you-like life as there are males who want to avoid the possibility of interrogation about why they weren't where they said would be.

The odd thing is, they still get involved with others and almost always with somebody who is eager to get their toothbrushes into the same bathroom as soon as possible!

You might be a commitment phobic yourself, or you might be wondering if somebody with whom you are involved is... Either way, this chapter is for you. It's also for you if you're just looking at the moment, because it will help you to avoid looking too hard and too long in the wrong place. There's even a self-help method if you suffer from this phobia though you would have to *truly want* to be free from it... And unless you have a desire to grow old on your own (there's absolutely nothing wrong with that if you do) it's probably a good idea to do your best to get rid of it. There is much evidence to show that those who commit to sharing their life with another live longer and more happily than those who choose to stay single.

The signs

Most commitmentphobes are of the **Nomad** personality, but that doesn't mean that all Nomad types are a bad bet, only that there are more who seek to avoid commitment in this personality group than in the other two. The six main signs are that they:

- Go off the radar every so often and you can't contact them.
- Are unreliable, sometimes not turning up for a date.
- Make plans that don't involve their partner without discussing them.
- Evade questions about marriage or moving in together.
- Become less attentive if you get serious.
- Live in a minimalist, clutter-free environment.

The last one of those, living in a minimalist way, might not make sense until you realise they are behaving like a true Nomad, ready to travel light with not too much baggage to carry with them. The other five signs are immediately obvious and if your partner exhibits any four of them, don't plan on marriage anytime soon.

Sometimes, though, something really odd happens; the confirmed anti-commitment individual is caught unawares and... falls in love. You might think that would fix things, but you'd be wrong. All that happens is, they move into a different stage of non-commitment, where they remain in a relationship, are reasonably reliable, yet steadfastly refuse to acknowledge that they are in any way settled or content with the situation. If pressed, they will say something like: *"Well, nothing's for ever, is it?"* or maybe: *"One day at a time, that's what I always say. Who knows what's around the next corner? One day at a time..."*

To the partner it can feel as if they are keeping their options open – and they might well be – but it's far more likely that **fear** is stopping them from admitting that they are actually quite happy with the stability that surrounds them. They don't want to finalise anything, just in case... but they wouldn't be able to tell you what that 'just in case' was actually about. It's easy to become irritated if you're on the wrong end of this situation but it's important to remember something you've already seen a few times in this book: *We cannot choose what we feel, only what we do with what we feel.* It is every bit as difficult for the one who fears commitment to enter fully into it, as it is for the fully committed one to walk away from the relationship.

Fixing it

The good news is: if you suffer from commitment phobia and you truly want to fix it, it's possible and perhaps even with the information in this chapter (though professional help is sometimes needed.) The bad news is: if you are currently with somebody who exhibits this fear, there's nothing *you* can do to fix it, other than sit tight and hope they eventually realise what a good thing they are into with you. It happens. It's rare, and it doesn't always last, but it happens.

The rest of this chapter is about helping those who experience this fear to overcome the problem and look forward to the future. Before we start, you will need to have completed the exercise in the last chapter, on creating your Virtual Personas and word pairs that serve as triggers to help you access the resources associated with each. We're assuming here that you already have your three profile sheets and that you are able to either see the Personas clearly in your mind's eye or you can vividly imagine them in some other way that works for you. It's important that you are able to readily bring to mind how they look, sound, smell and feel, as well as how they move around, so that you can recognise them just as certainly as if they were real people. Many people, in fact, become so familiar with these personas that, although they know they are just part of their imagination, they feel as if they know everything about them. Not just how they look, but also how they actually *are*.

The exercises you are going to do here require the highest level of realism in your Personas that you can imagine, even if they are fantasy characters, such as an ancient Chinese magician or a Sci-Fi Warrior. Because you have this commitment issue it is almost certain that you have a highly creative imagination – use it, and make those Personas truly vivid!

The method of working will depend on your dominant personality type, which you discovered in **Chapter Two** – and if you feel that might have changed as a result of what you've read since then, it's a good idea to go back and re-evaluate before working on this particular exercise. No harm will come to you if you were to work with the 'wrong' method but you might not get the best result out of it. There are also a couple of things to be aware of before you start.

- If you are eager to get started, this is a very good sign and an indicator that you have a good chance of finding success through these pages.
- If, on the other hand, you are feeling a kind of depressive certainty that it's not going to work, then it's odds-on that you need professional help. **Chapter Seventeen** – *can therapy help?* will help you find it.

Warrior

If you're a Warrior suffering from commitment fear, it's entirely possible that you are not so much frightened of commitment but of somehow relinquishing control of your life. It is entirely possible, though, that you've experienced some sort of traumatic situation in the past that has negatively coloured your view of how relationships actually work. It's even likely that you've accessed it already in some way, while reading the first two or three chapters of this book. One of the major sources is parental break up, especially if it was acrimonious or if you observed great difficulties befalling either parent as a result. If this happened in your life and you still feel anger or sadness about it, then it's possible that you recognise it to be the cause of your own resistance to commitment.

Remember, though, that you are not your parents and anybody you become involved with is not either of your parents. You are two entirely unique individuals. And anyway, history does *not* 'repeat itself' – it can't, it's done, finished, and it's in the past. It's nothing more than a neatly poetic phrase that some writer or other bandied around once. All that can happen sometimes is that a similar event happens... but precisely because you're sensitised to it, you are protected from it. You would see the signs long before things became serious and take steps to avoid the problem altogether. *This book shows you how!*

It's time for the Persona exercise now. You'll need to remember the gist of it, since you'll have your eyes closed. First, make sure you won't be disturbed for around thirty minutes or so and put your telephone on 'silent'. Then:

Find yourself a comfortable place to sit and relax but don't lay down or you'll probably go to sleep! Close your eyes, keeping them closed for the entire session, and breathe steadily for a few moments, just listening to the sound of your breathing until you feel a kind of still calmness. Think of your word pair for the Warrior, then let the image of the Persona come to mind and say, in your mind (out loud if you wish): *"Can you accept that I am safe in my relationship with ———?"*

If you experience a strong *"No!"* response, you can abandon this exercise, since it is evidence that it is not going to work. Either the relationship is *not* sound and your subconscious knows it, or your fear is deep-rooted enough that you will need professional help, as detailed in **Chapter Seventeen** – *Can therapy help?* to overcome the problem. You will do yourself no harm by continuing but that Warrior part of your psyche is so determined to keep you unattached that it is unlikely to work well.

Assuming you found a *"Yes"* response, however reluctant, you can proceed now by thanking the Warrior, then thinking of the word pair for first the Settler, then for the Nomad. Bring the Virtual Personas vividly to mind and imagine they are sharing your space – the more vivid you can make this the better, even if it feels slightly spooky. Say to them in your mind (or out loud if you wish): *"Warrior has agreed I am safe and I want you to help me actually feel it for myself. Will you do that?"* A *"No"* response is almost unheard of here but if you find it, then accept it as, again, an indicator from your subconscious mind that professional help is needed to discover what it is that is so fearful for you – and it *can* be resolved.

Assuming that you get an agreement, thank each Virtual Persona and then just allow whatever emotional response you feel to grow and become part of you. Glory in it and allow it to fill as much of your mind and body as you can, so that you become familiar with it. When you feel that you've managed to start making a real change, just allow your eyes to open.

Your personality is quite prone to habituation and to avoid this pulling you back again, you will need to do a small five-minute exercise each day for a while. It's simple though: close your eyes, think of the word pairs and bring all three Virtual Personas into your mind, and allow the Settler and Nomad to generate those same feelings once again. You should do this on a daily basis until you discover that you can find those wonderful feelings even without closing your eyes. Then you're done!

Settler

Settlers seldom suffer from commitment fear so it's possible that your real problem is that your partner will discover the truth – that you're not 'all that', nothing special at all, and simply cannot live up to what they seem to be thinking of you. Well, you're making a rather arrogant mistake here! That's not a very nice word, of course, but the fact is that you are assuming that you *know* that your partner just isn't able to see the real you! Of course, it's not real arrogance, but a fear that they will suddenly wake up to the fact that you're actually rather ordinary... but supposing they know that already? Supposing 'ordinary' is exactly what they've been looking for all their life, rather than somebody who is outrageously personable, sexy and charismatic, or a controlling individual who makes a habit of determinedly seeing the downside of everything?

It's what *they* think of you that counts to them, not what *you* think of you! Enjoy the fact that you're loved and wanted and if you insist on believing that you're just not what they think you are, then glory in your good luck that you have found somebody whose perception is 'not all that'!

Your exercise is an easy one, though you will need to memorise it first, as you'll be doing it with your eyes closed. First, make sure you won't be disturbed for a while, put your phone on silent and find a comfortable place to sit. Then:

Close your eyes and allow a sense of calm quietness to find its way into your mind and body, and when you have a still feeling, think of each word pair in turn, allowing each persona to come vividly to mind as you do so. When you can actually *feel* their presence in some way, ask this question in your mind, or out loud if you want to: *"Will you help me to always find the best in my life with ———?"* You are likely to feel a *"Yes"* response straight away but if not, continue with: *"Will you look after me all the time I am with ————?"* It is impossible to get anything other than a *"Yes"* answer to this question (because it's coming from your own subconscious, which wants to keep you safe) and you can allow your feelings for your partner to fill every pore of your being. Once a Settler has come to a realisation, there is seldom a need to repeat the process, but you can simply repeat the same exercise if you should feel the need to do so for any reason.

It is important to recognise that if any part of this exercise feels uncomfortable it is an indicator that all might not be well in your relationship. Of the three personality groups, you are the one who finds it easiest to love and trust... but you are also blessed with amazing intuition and it might be that you need to listen carefully to it. It won't let you down!

Nomad

Your inherited instincts are those of the traveller, so in many ways it's not really a surprise that you tend to be anxious about the idea of committing yourself to one person, one home, one life... In fact, many of your deepest instincts will rebel sharply at the idea, even though you might not be aware why this should be. The Nomad never did want to be fettered or held back – there was a wish to be free, to escape difficulty at the drop of a hat, to grab opportunity when it makes itself available, to take a new lover for a day or a month before moving on... Not for them the hearth and slippers!

There is a problem though, in that none of us are totally Nomad. There are always influences of the Warrior who wants to put down roots of stability and a Settler that just wants to be loved. This can create an uncomfortable conflict when the predominantly Nomad individual finds themselves involved with somebody who ticks all the boxes as far as providing stability and/or loving attention is concerned. At first, the opportunity for regular sexual activity and the comfort of sharing life and bed is rewarding enough to make the idea of staying in one place almost acceptable... but only almost. Boredom sets in with the passage of time and the Nomad starts to experience itchy feet, after which it's not long before the desire for new surroundings and a new lover begin to override any idea of domesticity and a monogamous life.

But many Nomad types gradually realise that no matter where they travel or who they're with, there's always that thought in the background that there might be something or someone better, more exciting, just around the corner. *The* one. The one who somehow manages to override the boredom and the same old same old aspects of everyday life.

If this is you, you really only have two choices: 1. Live like a Nomad of old, and don't even think about permanent relationships; or 2. Accept that while you're searching for your ideal situation, you might miss out on something wonderful and seek to change.

In the case of 1 (above) there's no real need for you to read the rest of this chapter but it's important to take on board the fact that you will inevitably cause pain for others if you make promises you won't keep. In the second instance though, you can create the change you need by strengthening the influence of both the Warrior and Settler elements of your personality. You will still be fun-loving, still enthusiastic and still optimistic, but you will be able to keep your feet on the ground when you need to. It's definitely a win-win situation!

You'll need to memorise this exercise because you'll be doing it with your eyes closed to help you use that powerful imagination of yours more vividly. Make sure you won't be disturbed for around thirty minutes or so (though you might not actually need that long) and set your mobile to 'silent' so calls, emails or texts messages won't interrupt you. Then:

Close your eyes and imagine for a few moments that you can breathe in through your fingers and out through your feet, so it's as if you can feel a single warming flow of air travelling through your entire body. Allow a calmness to settle around you and then think of your word pairs, one at a time, creating an image of the associated Virtual Persona as you do so. When you have them all in your mind, look at the Nomad and imagine, as vividly as you can, that he or she is impatiently restless, itching to move on to somewhere more exciting. When you can see it, let yourself actually *feel* it – it's a sensation that's familiar to you so it's an easy task.

Now see the Warrior and Settler each place a hand on the Nomad, perhaps on the shoulder or arm; the Settler is gentle, sending a feeling of affectionate love into your whole being, while the Warrior is giving you a sense of stability and strength. You can see the softness of the one and the sheer strength of the other, and you can allow that feeling to flow through your entire body with each breath you take, still imagining breathing in through your fingers and out through your feet. Continue with this for a while until it starts to seem rather ordinary, then allow your eyes to open.

You'll need to do that exercise every day for a while until it becomes difficult to conjure up those impatiently restless feelings in the Nomad. What that will mean is that you have gained confidence in your ability to create exactly what you want around you without travelling in search of it. After that, you can do the same exercise if you ever get those restless feelings but want to 'stay put'. It's your choice. Nobody can *make* you do it, which is what makes it so powerful. You are every bit as much of a free spirit as you've always been, doing things by choice because you want to, not because somebody else is pressuring you in some way or seeking to control you with some threat or other. In other words, you will still be your own person, doing your own thing – it's just that you'll have a much easier life while you do it!

A final thought

It's important to bear in mind that some Nomads will never be able to adopt a static existence and have absolutely no wish to even try it. If that's you, just accept that you are made that way and you shouldn't allow anybody to clip your wings unless you have a change of heart (which is a possibility.) And if you suspect that your partner fits into this mould, then enjoy the relationship and accept it for what it is – fun, exciting, but probably short-lived. If you keep that in mind, you won't hurt so badly when it comes to an end.

Chapter Sixteen

Common problems, uncommon answers

A lot of this chapter is about sex, mainly because a great many difficulties in relationships either stem *from* sexual problems or lead to them. A lot of the time, the couple is not fully aware – or perhaps turn from the awareness – that their difficulties are sexually related and, instead of solving them, they split up. The big problem is that the same issue so often reappears in the next relationship, or the one after, and can eventually lead to psychological difficulties, including depression or anxiety.

There are many other problems that a couple might face, of course, but since this book is about love and sex, that's the focus of attention here. We'll look at a few of the non-sexual difficulties first, though it's fair to say that any one of those could eventually 'infect' the sex life of the couple. It's also worth reading **Chapters Four** and **Five** again, since they cover a lot of ground that is relevant to the sort of problems that might be encountered.

The 'wrong' partner

This first situation has more to do with what goes on *before* a relationship than what happens within it. We've all seen examples of it, in the individual who seems to have the most appalling luck when it comes to relationships, always ending up with somebody who is totally unsuitable for one reason or another. Females with this 'syndrome' find themselves with men who turn out to be violent, alcohol-dependent, excessively controlling, gamblers, wasters, philanderers or worse. Males discover their mate to be a spendthrift, unfaithful, lazy, frigid, manipulative, disinterested or any one of several other uncomfortable traits. In almost all cases, the individual who always gets this raw deal believes they attract the 'wrong type of person'.

They spend ages talking to friends and family about why this should be and even if they come to some conclusion – the clothes they wear, the way they speak, the places they go, for instance – and make changes, the same thing continues to happen. They *still* end up with a partner who is never going to help them find the happiness they seek. Quite the opposite, in fact.

The reason most are not able to resolve the issue is not really a mystery, even though it might seem like it – it's that they're looking in the wrong direction. The truth is that they *do not* 'attract the wrong type of person', but that they are *attracted to* 'the wrong type of person' and send out unconscious signals that say so! When you think about it, it's the only solution that makes sense. The one common factor in all the unsuitable relationships is the person who experiences them – the other parties are all different from each other, though they will have one common factor which is what draws the attention of the unfortunate serial 'wrong partner getter'.

You might remember reading in **Chapter Three** *– The way people are and the games they play, how we are all experts at reading how others function, even if we don't realise it. We pick up the almost invisible indicators of a type that for some reason appeals sexually, because that's what the attraction is. It might be rogue or tart, aloof or needy, wild or innocent; it might be something we grew up with or something we yearned for while growing up; it might based on a parent or other relative or even the next-door neighbour. But whatever it is, the person with this syndrome sees it, wants, and sends out the signals to get it.*

This problem is resolvable, though not really within this scope of this book, being better dealt with by a professional therapist (**Chapter Seventeen** *– Can therapy help?* will tell you more about that.) But if you fall into this category, you can now begin to examine what it might be that attracts you and recognise it as 'toxic', and you can also attempt to discover how you actually send out those 'I want YOU!' signals. Finding and understanding those two elements is often enough to fix the problem, though a therapist might help you discover why you had them in the first place. It is a fact that discovering where that urge comes from is usually enough on its own to completely change the type of person an individual will be attracted to.

Every relationship dies

This is a different situation altogether, in that everything seems to start off perfectly well but then somehow or another just fades away. There are three possibilities to consider:

- It's usually you who 'cools off' or loses interest.
- It's usually your partner who decides it's over.
- It's usually a mutual decision.

Because there are different energies and 'dynamics' associated with each situation, we'll look at them individually.

Usually you: This can be based on many things, including commitment fear/phobia – the subconscious is absolutely brilliant at operating protection of self, and a possible way it can work is to simply have you tiring of the latest 'flame'. Sometimes, it might be fear of your preferred gender that creates the subconscious anxiety in the first place. The previous chapter has some information that will help you deal with this situation.

Of course, it might be that you have the 'template' of the ideal partner in mind and though it seems you have found them at first, you gradually come to realise that they are lacking in some way. Usually, this means that they *look* right and superficially *seem* right... But as you get to know them, there are habits, attitudes, and behaviour patterns that just don't sit well with you. If this keeps on happening, it suggests that you might have unrealistic expectations, though since they are coming from your subconscious and are based on what you learnt as 'truth', while you were a child, it probably doesn't feel like that at all. It can be very difficult to just decide to change, though some of the other chapters in this book might well help. As a guide, anywhere you find yourself being surprised at what you're reading is worth thinking about in depth.

Usually your partner: This is usually related to 'always choosing the wrong partner' (above) and is likely to do with what can be thought of as 'false advertising.' In other words, the 'you' that you project during the exploratory phase of a relationship (which includes the first time you meet, before you even know each other's names) is not the same as the 'you' that begins to show as the relationship matures. For reasons best known to yourself, or your subconscious, you are projecting an image that you believe the other person is looking for... Which is pointless, since you will never be able to sustain it for a lifetime!

All the time you project what you think is important to somebody else, you will never find the person who would truly love the real you. Instead you will continue to attract people who go for what you show them in the beginning then leave when they discover there was no substance underneath the promise. *Pretending you are anything that you actually are not, including sexual appetite and/or ability, is a recipe for disaster!* For the other person, it's just like when you buy something where the advertising gives you a thrill but the actual product immediately disappoints you. Be you, be real, and find the partner that will love you for it.

There is one other possibility and that is that there is some physical problem that only becomes obvious during the relationship. There are a whole host of possibilities here, including personal hygiene, toilet habits, eating manners (mouth open, noisy, messy, and so on), sleeping habits, slovenliness and other things like them. If partners tend to criticise you about any of these or similar things, do have a long think before you dismiss it as unfair. Remember – that **Sexy/Unsexy** balance can be affected adversely by any of them.

Usually mutual: This is a complex issue though certainly a fairly well known one, and the roots of it are more often than not in the subconscious of one or both partners. It's always difficult to tell, since it tends to be infectious, as off the wall as that might sound. It's all about belief and expectation, both of them very powerful forces in the mind. If only one half of a couple believes from the outset that something is bound to go wrong, then they will act and behave accordingly. In a dozen almost invisible ways, they will convey this to their partner and in a dozen almost invisible ways the partner will pick it up... and can easily begin to think you're not keen on staying in the relationship.

Before you dismiss the whole idea, here are just a few examples of the sort of thing that can work as signals: *staring fixedly straight ahead when walking past a jewellers; checking out other individuals; overt submissive behaviour; quiet moods for no good reason; avoiding conversation about the relationships of others; shaking your head 'no' when asking a question you would clearly like a 'yes' to; reluctance to discuss the future*

There are many more signals of this sort and you can rest assured that if you have a belief that the relationship may not last, it will act as a self-fulfilling prophecy. If you believe it and expect it, the subconscious will assume that you want it and will obligingly communicate that fact to your partner. It can even look like a fear of commitment. BUT... It's possible that you are picking up these signals from your partner in the first place and reacting to them. There's no real way of knowing and the only thing you can do is a kind of damage limitation exercise where, all the time you want it to be, you assume that this relationship is at least semi-permanent and then your subconscious will give you an entirely different set of signals. It's not foolproof though and if your partner wants out at any time, you'll soon become aware of it. But at least you'll know that it wasn't any of your doing... probably.

Constant arguments

When constant arguments blight every relationship you're in, there can only be one reason... You're argumentative! Now, you might strongly disagree with that (but it would only prove to illustrate the point perhaps) on the basis that it's not you who starts the arguments. The term 'argumentative' is often misunderstood, though; it really just means that somebody is prone to argue and it doesn't matter who or what starts it off – if you disagree with somebody then you're being argumentative and if they disagree back then you *both* are. There's no suggestion that this is a bad thing or that being argumentative is in any way a negative attitude, only that if this is your nature and you are with somebody else who is similar, then it is a fact of life.

It's not a 'relationship killer' as long as you accept that it means nothing more than that two people can be close enough to vigorously disagree yet continue to love each other. The secret of surviving happily in this situation is to keep to the subject of the argument, rather than letting it spread into a hundred-and-one (or more!) other areas of life. **Chapter Nine** – *Arguing in a straight line* has a lot more to say about this sort of issue.

Money

This is a tough one. It is often said that sex and money are the biggest causes of arguments in a relationship, and that probably *is* the case. There are three main possibilities here:

- There just isn't enough money.
- Your partner spends too much.
- You spend too much.

Each situation carries its own complications and we'll consider each one separately:

Not enough: This is a joint situation and not one that can be resolved by arguments. In fact, the only way you can approach this is with calm conversation about how to either increase income or cut outgoings. Recriminations and accusations will only serve to create conflict and that means you will then be on opposite sides of the fence arguing *against* each other instead of on the same side of the fence planning *with* each other. No matter what the cause, a constructive discussion is the only answer, be it about getting a new job, finding an extra income, cutting down on luxury items, raiding the savings or anything else. It's something you have to solve together if you want to stay together.

Partner spends too much: The key here is to keep anger, recrimination, criticism and sarcasm as far out of the way as possible, because as soon as they come into the frame you run the risk of triggering antagonism. You can rave, shout and throw the most enormous tantrum, and your partner might make a change, though it's unlikely to last. The best approach is always conversational: *"I know you like buying things but we need to find a way of keeping up with the expense..."* is a good opening gambit. Explore the situation and keep on exploring it until your partner comes to the conclusion that there isn't any practical way of doing that. This *might* create a lasting change but only if they genuinely hadn't realised their spending habits were leading to financial disaster. Even then, there's always a risk involved – often, once a spender always a spender – so you need some sort of 'management plan' in order to keep safe, though this must be agreed by both of you. This one is probably the trickiest of all situations to change, since you're on the outside and cannot force a change of behaviour into somebody else's mind.

You spend too much

At least you have a chance of getting to grips with this more easily than if it's your partner who overspends – especially if nothing has been said yet. It's a good sign that you are aware of the problem. If, though, you are convinced that the reality is that your partner is trying to rein in your spending and that in reality you are completely within your means, then you need to do a 'financial analysis' of incomings and outgoings. Boring, yes, but irresponsible and potentially disastrous to refuse. Shutting your eyes and covering your ears whilst singing loudly won't make the problem go away! Anyway, you might discover that you were right all along... But if not, then you have to be fair and work at a management plan if you don't want to hurt your relationship.

If your problem is the over-use of credit cards then the old solution of plonking *every one of them* into a jug of water and putting it in the freezer can work well. By the time they've thawed out, the buying impulse has had the chance to settle down a little – and if you're going out especially to buy something, price it up first and stick to your target. And to be sure to avoid *unplanned* purchases!

Alcohol

This problem is really out of the scope of this book and is only mentioned because it's a hugely destructive influence. The sad truth is that somebody who suffers from alcohol dependence – and *both* partners suffer, really – will seldom change until they've truly hit rock bottom. It's not sufficient to just believe that they will do so if they carry on drinking. It has to actually happen, with few exceptions. If you find yourself with somebody with this problem who loves you to distraction, the kindest thing you can do is leave them but with the information that if they get dry, you'll try again. It's about the only thing that might give them enough of an initiative to stop, though it's unlikely they'll be able to do so on their own, needing professional help and support to get them to stay dry. This can be by specific organisations such as Alcoholics Anonymous, of course, or private one-to-one therapy.

The next chapter explains more about how to ensure that any

therapist who is approached is competent.

Sexual Problems

There are a great many sexual difficulties but here, we are covering the ones most likely to cause a rift in an otherwise viable relationship. For this reason, we are not looking at paedophilia, transgender, gender confusion, cross-dressing, perversions (properly called *fetishes* or *paraphilias)*, sado-masochism, bondage or any of the other extremes of sexual behaviour. They are all complex issues that would need a lot more specialist attention than this book can provide, and it is also rare that these unfortunate individuals find themselves in a 'normal' relationship.

The issues we are looking at here (besides those covered in **Chapter Five** – *What the other half doesn't know... about sex*) are:

Erectile Dysfunction
Performance Anxiety
Vaginismus
Vulvadynia
Anorgasmia
Frigidity
Use of pornography
Serial infidelity

As usual in this book, we'll examine each of those concepts individually, though not necessarily in great detail – it would need an entire book the size of this one to do that alone! That said, there's enough information to help you find more assistance if you need to.

Erectile Dysfunction (ED)

Most men will experience this from time to time and it is important that their partner should not make too big a deal out of the situation – it is a well-established fact that pressure makes the problem worse. Many people believe it to be mainly a psychological problem, whereas it is actually a physical problem four times out of five. For this reason, a responsible therapist will not work with this problem until medical advice has been sought – and most of the time there is a medical answer to the problem.

ED can be caused by: *High blood pressure, low testosterone, diabetes, kidney disease, prostate cancer, prostatitis, prostate removal, circulatory problems, vitamin deficiencies, hormonal issues, alcohol abuse, smoking tobacco, some medication, atherosclerosis, drug abuse, being drunk, anxiety, penetration fear, tiredness.* Whatever its cause, it is always distressing for a man. Biologically, the very reason for his existence is his ability to make a female pregnant and if he loses that ability, the result can be profound depression. (The nearest equivalent for a female, though it's not the same, is being infertile.)

The most important thing for a male who suffers this problem for longer than a month or so is to visit his GP to discuss it. There's no need for embarrassment – it's something that medical professionals are extremely familiar with and the sooner treatment is sought, the sooner normal lovemaking can resume.

Performance anxiety

This can affect males or females and has sometimes been described as 'sexual stage fright'. It can be caused by any number of usually fear-based situations. Fear of: *Partner, humiliation, inability to climax, looking ugly, sounding ridiculous, being ineffective* and other irrational worries. Conversation with a loving and patient partner can help enormously, whereas professional help can be faster.

Vaginismus

Sometimes presenting as penetration fear, this is where the muscles of the vagina go into a spasm as soon as any attempt at intercourse is made. She will typically be convinced that there's something wrong 'down there' though such a situation is extremely rare. She usually has no difficulty with arousal though if it's for sex, rather than masturbation, she might not lubricate very well, if at all. Interestingly, many women with this problem are averse to masturbation and this can be part of the problem, especially if she believes that sex and sexual arousal are in some way 'dirty'. This is a problem that can sometimes be solved with a loving and patient partner and plenty of lubricating gel, though professional help is more certain to be effective – and in the vast majority of cases, totally successful.

The first action is to consult with a gynaecologist to confirm that there is no physical issue, then a therapist with experience of working with this problem.

Vulvadynia

A fairly rare condition, this inhibits sexual intercourse because of pain whenever there is an attempt. There is seldom any initial spasm of the vaginal muscles, unlike Vaginismus, and medical investigation doesn't usually reveal the reason for the pain, which is generally in the *Vestibule*, just inside the vaginal opening. This condition was originally known as *Vestibulitis*, though the 'itis' part of that name is an indicator of inflammation. Because there is no inflammation involved, it was renamed 'Vulvadynia', referring to pain in and around the vulva, or pubis. The bad news is that there doesn't appear to be any reliable 'cure' for the condition and it is not known what causes it, though it *might* be psychosomatic. A therapist, therefore, might have a better chance of resolving the problem than the doctor has, though a gynaecologist should always be the first port of call.

Anorgasmia

Put simply, this is the inability to achieve sexual climax, though it's not unusual for the problem to be only associated with sexual intercourse, masturbation producing perfectly fine orgasms. This is not to say that the problem is with the male, though it might be; but it can be the case that there is more than adequate foreplay, enough time taken during intercourse itself, the 'right' sort of intercourse (rough, gentle, loving, tantric or whatever), and yet the female still cannot achieve orgasm except by the use of fingers, a vibrator or other 'toy'.

The problem can be psychological, or it can be just that the male's body doesn't contact the female pubis in quite the right place to provide enough pressure and stimulation to the clitoral area, which is essential. Many males believe the 'pleasure centres' are in the vagina and that is therefore where they have to do their 'job'. In those cases – and conversation will reveal if this is so – a little education can produce a wondrous result! All he needs to do, sometimes, is to make sure that he adjusts his position slightly so that he's concentrating on the pubis rather than the vagina. Getting his lower belly rubbing that area can work wonders for some females but when all else fails, he can learn to be a gentleman and do whatever his partner needs him to do to produce an orgasm.

An associated problem is that the female orgasm often seems more important to the male than it does to her. The evolutionary reasons for this are unclear (but then again, the same applies to the female orgasm itself) but many women believe it's simply an ego 'thing'. There may be an element of truth here with *some* males but the major reason, without any doubt whatsoever, is that he finds the female orgasm hugely erotic. Some women believe they look ugly during those moments – which can be one of the reasons for the inability to climax during intercourse – and yet, once again, the female's facial expression as she approaches, then reaches, orgasm is a highly erotic experience for the male. So much is this the case that the female who makes the right sound and facial expression, at the same time squeezing her pelvic floor muscles and tightening her clasp around her lover will create a completion of intercourse almost immediately. Not that it should ever be suggested that she might do that just to get it over and done with sometimes...

Frigidity

True frigidity is fairly rare and glories in the professional name of 'Hypoactive Desire Disorder' – in other words, a lack of sexual drive or interest. Many males use the expression 'frigid' as a kind of insult, as if it were a deliberate choice. Yet she has no control over it, any more than the male has control over his instant recognition that he 'would' or 'would not' have sex with any woman he meets. Frigidity can have its roots in a physiological difficulty or might be of psychological origin, possibly as a result of a long-forgotten event (not necessarily sexual and not necessarily traumatic). The biggest problem is that it is quite difficult to diagnose which of the two possibilities is the source of the problem. For this reason, a consultation with a gynaecologist or sexual health clinic is indicated, followed by a meeting with a suitable therapist if nothing untoward is found. The success rate is not especially high with this problem, though it is far from unknown for full libidic interest to awaken with the right style of therapy.

Use of pornography

This is only a problem if one partner likes porn and the other abhors it – and those who like it will always seeks ways to observe it clandestinely if their partner is angrily disapproving. Many females view the male interest, quite understandably, as akin to infidelity, yet to the male it feels like nothing of the sort. To him, it is nothing more than fantasy, masturbation material perhaps, and no more like an affair than looking at a photograph of a naked female in the newspaper. To her, it can feel as if he is 'window shopping' for a mistress. Males have always had, and always will have for many thousand of years yet, an unquenchable urge to look at the female form. He has no choice in the matter (though most would fiercely resist it being taken from them) and most are content to just look with no real urge to engage in physical intercourse – the fantasy is sufficient. A sensible male, if his partner disapproves, will keep any use of porn discreet; a sensible female will allow him to do just that, rather than pry into his Internet browsing history.

None of this is as exclusively a male concept as might be imagined – there are many women who enjoy looking at porn, though are not necessarily overjoyed at the idea of their partner knowing about this. One of the experiments into sexuality that were carried out late in the twentieth century at Johns Hopkins University, USA, arrived at a surprising result: females watching porn would climax faster than most men, averaging just over two minutes from 'cold'. This, of course, gives the lie to the belief that foreplay is *always* necessary; sufficient excitation and arousal can occur for the same reason as for males – there is somebody sexy who they're not familiar with doing sexy 'stuff'. This is the subconscious procreative urge in action, seeking to breed with different partners so that not all the offspring will share any common genetic defect.

Of course, nobody thinks about that consciously. It is a process that has evolved via the mechanism of evolution; those who bred with the most people were more likely than most to produce healthy children... who also inherited the genetic tendency to seek multiple partners. Which leads rather nicely on to our next subject...

Serial infidelity

Because of the social and moral code in the Western part of the world, most people make at least *some* effort to keep the human tendency to 'do it' with several different partners under control. Others, however, will only pay lip service to this – and some won't even bother to do that. It's not just males, as some might imagine, but also a good few 'huntress' females.

It's fair to say that the majority of people in a reasonably comfortable relationship won't *actively seek* to have an affair. When it happens, it is much more likely that they have encountered a situation where there is a powerful animal attraction (there's more about this in **Chapter Thirteen** – *What's love got to do with it?*) that has overridden the 'responsibility switches' for long enough to get as far as sexual intercourse. If that consummation is better than they have previously experienced, they are then hooked, at least until the excitement of a new partner has faded, which it inevitably does. Sometimes though, there might well be an emotional involvement by then to sustain the situation.

Serial infidelity, though, is a different matter altogether. What happens in this situation certainly doesn't happen by chance or accident. The serial philanderer *seeks* sexual partners for a 'fling' and certainly doesn't want a lasting relationship – though, oddly perhaps, they will try to sustain exactly that with their 'full time' partner, promising over and again that they will mend their ways. This situation is actually a form of abuse for which there are few, if any, answers. This might be an illness like sexual obsession or sexual addiction but it's one for which any 'cure' is often unreliable. If you suffer from this situation yourself and you want to fix it, there's help in the next chapter, though only in so far as it will advise how best to find a therapist to work with you, since it is beyond the scope of this book. If you have discovered that your partner has the problem, then you really only have three choices:

- Accept that this is the way your life is likely to continue.
- Tell your partner – and mean it – that it's over unless they get help.
- Leave and start a new life, using the information in this

book to help you.

It is to be hoped that if you are experiencing any of the problems covered in this chapter you are a little more informed and have some idea of how to find help. On the other hand, if you've been just looking, then forewarned is forearmed...

Chapter Seventeen

Can therapy help?

There is no suggestion that any of the organisations mentioned here are the best or in some way preferred, only that they are known to be reputable and might be able to help with your difficulty. Most 'mind therapies' are currently not regulated in the same way as conventional medicine, though they do have stringent requirements for registration with the associated professional bodies. A powerful self-therapy methodology is included at the end of this chapter.

Something to take on board straight away here is that if you present for therapy of any sort, it is of enormous importance that you feel confident and at ease with the therapist. It doesn't matter how many people tell you that 'John Brown' is a brilliant and highly qualified individual, or how many recommendations and testimonials he has on his website, if you don't like him *therapy won't work!*

Always consider somebody if you get a personal recommendation, of course, but insist on an initial consultation before agreeing to any therapy. Trust your instincts – they will assess a therapist just as well as they will anybody else! Therapists are not special people, and might not even be especially clever, though they do have specialised knowledge as a rule. If, after a meeting, you like them and feel confident they can help you, then that's when to make your appointment for work to begin. On the other hand, if you have any misgivings, however slight, just say politely that you'd like to think about it and take your leave of them.

There are several different types of therapy for the mind, each with advantages and disadvantages. We'll look at a few of the different disciplines (types of therapy) in this chapter, along with advice as to what they might help with. It's worth noting that psychiatry and psychology are not included, since neither of those disciplines is ideally suited for the problems discussed in this book. The therapies covered in this chapter are:

- Counselling
- Psychotherapy
- Hypnotherapy
- Cognitive Behavioural Therapy
- Meridian therapies
- NLP (Neuro-Linguistic Programming)
- Self-therapy

A short description is given of each, certainly enough for you to understand how it might work for you and/or your partner, along with details that will allow you to find a therapist in your area.

Counselling

Many people mistakenly believe that this is the only 'real' form of therapy that is available and that it is good for just about any problem. Well, it's fair to say that a professional counsellor might well be able to work with almost any problem, though that certainly doesn't mean that it's the best or most suitable discipline for your needs. Counselling involves you doing far more talking than the counsellor, who usually will not recommend or suggest any answers for your presenting problem, instead guiding and allowing you to find the answers within yourself. There are several different styles of counselling and you can investigate them at this website: http://www.counselling-directory .org.uk/counselling.html where you can also find a counsellor near you.

- **Pros:** Accessible, often available on the National Health Service (in the UK), though with lengthy wait times, can work with many different issues, solid training. Private consultations from around £35.00 per fifty-minute session.

- **Cons:** Can take many sessions, perhaps years, to resolve some issues and even then may not always effect a full remission of the presenting problem.

Good for: Family difficulties, stress management, confidence issues, coping strategies, PTSD, grief and bereavement, some relationship issues, couples counselling, anger management, money problems.

Not best for: Sexual problems, alcohol or drug dependence, depression, repetitive destructive behaviour, anything where a fast result is needed.

Psychotherapy

Psychotherapy is similar to counselling in many ways, though generally, a psychotherapist will interact more with the client than would a counsellor. A common belief is that it's only intended for mentally disturbed individuals or those with very serious problems, and also that you must be referred by a conventional medical practitioner or consultant. None of this is accurate! Psychotherapy as a discipline can provide help for very many every day issues and there are a huge number of qualified professional therapists who work in the private sector – and if they're not excellent at what they do, they tend to not be able to stay in practice!

As with counselling, there are several different styles of working and this website will help you understand them: http://www.psychotherapy.org.uk/public.html There is also a register of professionally qualified therapists to choose from.

- **Pros:** Widely available, can work effectively with a wide range of issues, solid training, available on the National Health Service (in the UK) though with a considerable waiting time and limited number of sessions. Private consultations range from £50.00 upwards for a fifty-minute session.

- **Cons:** Can take many sessions (perhaps years) to resolve some issues.

Good for: Most emotional issues, anger management, stress relief, grief and bereavement, depression, PTSD, alcohol and other dependencies (with a specialist therapist), repetitive destructive behaviour, obsessive problems, jealousy, gambling problems.

Not best for: Sexual difficulties, money problems, family problems, relationship issues, anything where a fast result is needed.

Hypnotherapy

Described by some as 'turbo-charged psychotherapy' this can provide astonishingly fast relief for a huge number of difficulties. There are many misconceptions about this discipline though, chiefly that it embodies some form of mind control by the therapist, or that all sorts of things might happen to client while they are 'out of it' about which they would have no knowledge. In fact, there is no unconsciousness involved at all and many who experience this discipline are astonished to discover that their senses are actually heightened, so they are *more* aware of what's going on than they are in the usual way. Newspaper stories that suggest otherwise can safely be ignored, as can the occasional assertion that somebody has committed murder, robbery, sexual offences and more with the use of hypnosis. It sells newspapers but it's far from reality – in fact most people are concerned that they might not have 'gone under' during their sessions with a hypnotherapist, since there is no special 'hypnotised feeling' and they were aware of all that was going on around them.

There are a huge number of areas in which hypnotherapy can

be effective, probably more than any other style of 'mind work', and you can investigate it in detail at this website: http://www.hypnotherapy-directory.org.uk/ where you can also locate a hypnotherapist in your area. There is a difficulty with this discipline, though, in that it was at one time poorly regulated with enormously wide variations in training. This changed in 2010 with introduction of Voluntary Self Regulation and the majority of hypnotherapists are now competent. If they are registered with the Complementary and Natural Healthcare Council (CNHC) in the UK and Europe, you can rest assured they are professionally qualified and insured. You can search the register of CNHC at their website: http://www.cnhc.org.uk

As with counselling and psychotherapy, there are a few different 'models' of hypnotherapy available, including *Hypnoanalysis, Suggestion* and *Solution Focussed work.* Your hypnotherapist will be able to advise which is the best for your difficulty.

- **Pros:** Widely available, can work with a lot of different issues, usually faster than counselling or psychotherapy, can provide total alleviation of symptoms.
- **Cons:** Not available on most health insurances, not on the National Health Service, consultation prices and skill levels vary widely (and price does not necessarily reflect quality or experience.)

Good for: Habits, phobias, fears, stress-related issues, PTSD, anxiety, self-worth, self-confidence, sexual problems, relationship issues, grief and bereavement, anger management, jealousy, some depression, some addictions.

Not best for: OCD, alcohol dependence, drug addiction, gambling, couples therapy, money problems, family issues.

Cognitive Behavioural Therapy (CBT)

Essentially a form of psychotherapy, this has gathered approval from many quarters in the last few years, being considered an 'evidence-based' therapy. Approved by the National Health Service (in the UK) and by many, maybe most, health insurance companies this style of therapy is relatively brief. However, there is much empirical evidence to suggest that although early results of therapy are extremely promising, the alleviation of symptoms might not always be permanent.

It is a highly interactive therapy involving the client, in which belief structures and expectations will be examined and quite often challenged, to good effect – the client will often come to realise that their thoughts were the only source of their problems. There is quite a lot of homework for the client to complete in many cases, such as keeping notes of feelings and thoughts, and failure in this respect will limit the effectiveness of therapy. This is actually a good thing, since the client quickly learns to take responsibility for their own issues and finds the resources within themselves to deal with those issues. There is a downside in that the client might well have to remember to do certain 'thought exercises' after therapy is complete in order to maintain the results. This website explains it in detail: http://www.mind.org.uk/mental_health_a-z/8000_cognitive_behaviour_therapy

You will also be able to find a CBT practitioner at the same site.

- **Pros:** Available on the NHS, though with limited number of sessions; widely available, mostly sound training, faster than counselling or 'standard' psychotherapy, can provide an excellent reduction of symptoms. Reasonably priced at £45.00 upwards per session depending on geographical location.
- **Cons:** Not all practitioners have received formal training in

the discipline, skill levels vary widely, results *might* not be permanent.

Good for: Many issues including irrational thoughts or behaviours, self-worth issues, anxiety disorders, depression, PTSD, anger. Excellent therapy for OCD (Obsessive Compulsive Disorder)

Not best for: Relationship issues, sexual problems, family difficulties, money problems, alcohol and substance abuse/dependency, gambling.

Meridian Therapies

Meridian therapies are modern yet at the same time, ancient, employing pressure and/or tapping with the fingertips on the meridian points defined in ancient Chinese medicine and which have been in use in acupuncture and acupressure techniques in the Western world for some considerable time now. Here, we are looking at the two major types of this modern form of therapy, **EFT** *(Emotional Freedom Technique)* and **TFT** *(Thought Field Therapy)*. They are actually similar to each other in that both involve tapping or pressing on the meridian points around the body for a few seconds at a time, whilst repeating over and again a statement or affirmation associated with whatever is that is perceived to be in the way of whatever we want to achieve. The major difference between them is that in EFT therapy, the tapping is done on several meridian points consecutively, while in TFT it is usually on only specific points associated with the presenting problem.

Generally, it is the client who does the tapping, guided by the therapist; most of the points are 'mirrored' around the body (three of them on the head are central), so that you can tap with either hand on either side of the body – it doesn't seem to matter which, or even if you change sides half way through a session. It might sound strange, but can be hugely effective. Both techniques can be carried out entirely by telephone consultation – you do the tapping/pressing of Meridian therapy under instruction from the therapist.

This website tells you more and also has a list of registered practitioners for you to choose from: http://theamt.com

- **Pros:** Not available on insurance or the National Health Service, is often part of the services offered by psychotherapists, hypnotherapists and counsellors, therefore widely available, reasonably priced at around £50.00 – £60.00 per session for many practitioners.
- **Cons:** Might not address the underlying cause of your problems, might not provide a permanent cure on its own.

Good for: Phobias, fears, anxiety, depression, self-worth issues, destructive habits and thoughts, some sexual difficulties.

Not best for: Family issues, relationship problems, money issues, anger management, stress, habits such as smoking and nail biting.

NLP (Neuro-Linguistic Programming)

NLP is not generally held to be a model of therapy so much these days, as a methodology for personal development and business success. As such, it's not being covered in detail here and, in fact, is only mentioned because many people have heard of it and wonder if it could help them. This website: http://www.anlp.org will show you all that NLP is and what if can do, though it is generally not recommended for the issues covered in this book.

Self-therapy

Literally millions of people around the world have benefited hugely from various forms of self-therapy – and you've already experienced quite a bit within these pages whenever you've done any of the **Warriors, Settlers** and **Nomads** exercises. There's nothing mysterious or complicated about providing therapy for self; all it needs is something to fascinate the subconscious mind followed by a focus on whatever you want to achieve. Without doubt, the most powerful form of self-therapy is self-hypnosis and that is what we're going to be looking at here – first, though, here are just a few words to dispel any fears about the process:

- You cannot 'get stuck' – this is totally impossible.
- You cannot lose your mind or identity – this is also totally impossible.
- There's no such thing as a 'hypnotised feeling', so it feels ordinary or as if nothing's happening.
- Because of that last one, you might think you were unsuccessful.
- Only when you open your eyes will you be aware that 'something was different'.
- You might go into a deep state or only light. It doesn't matter which.
- You can come out of hypnosis whenever you decide to.
- You will be totally aware of everything going on around you.

The most important thing about it is to work to a structured format:

- Decide what you want to happen as a result of the work and write it down as a suggestion, using as few words as possible (you'll need to remember it!)
- Be sure to say what you *do* want, rather than what you *do not* want: *I don't want to keep feeling anxious about relationships* is not the same, to the subconscious, as: *From now on I will begin to feel more confident about relationships.* Begin your suggestion with 'From now on I will...' If you prefer it, you can use: *I want to feel steadily more confident...* which

removes any 'time pressure' you might have otherwise experienced.

- Imagine exactly how your life will be when you have achieved your goal, how that goal *feels, smells, looks* and *sounds*. This is known as the 'four sense' test and you can apply it to almost any goal. Be sure to remember it.

- If you are a **Warrior,** work at the idea of being more in control of your life; if you are a **Settler,** think about how you will seem closer to others; if you are a **Nomad,** work at the idea of being impressive to others.

- Work on one thing at a time and only move on to something else when you've achieved your goal. Trying to achieve two or more goals at the same time might confuse the subconscious into doing nothing!

- During the session, repeat your suggestion as many times as you like – there is no upper limit – and keep focussed on every aspect of it.

- As you repeat your suggestion, be sure to visualise or imagine as best you can the four sense test you created in your structure.

There are many ways to achieve a state of self-hypnosis, some of them lengthy and requiring you to record them to listen to later. They work, but the method given here is easy to remember and every bit as effective. As with one or two of the other exercises you've done, you'll need to memorise it, but it's not difficult. Make sure you won't be disturbed for around thirty minutes or so, switch your phone to silent, sit yourself down in a comfortable place and close your eyes, then:

Breathe steadily for a few moments, listening to the sound of each breath in and out, and when you feel a stillness, imagine yourself being surrounded by a cocoon of your favourite colour. After a little while imagine, think or guess what scent that colour might have... Then, in your mind's ear, hear a musical sound that might go with the scent and colour – it can be a series of notes or just a single tone, like a temple bell, for instance. Finally let yourself imagine what that those three things together might feel like in or on your body if you were actually able to feel it. (You might have already recognised that this is the 'four sense test' again but it doesn't actually matter whether you are excellent at it, or struggle a bit – it's the focussing on it that produces the inward looking state that is ideal for the type of work you are doing here. It also prepares your mind for what comes next.)

When you are completely at ease with this and can comfortably sustain the thought or imagination of the colour, scent, sound and feel, say your suggestion to yourself – aloud is best but in your mind is acceptable if you feel self-conscious. Each time you say it, imagine or think of the four senses associated with it. Continue with this until you get a feeling that you've done enough for today then just pause and allow quietness and stillness to fill your body for a little while. Just listen to your breathing without thinking any more about your suggestion, the colours, scents, sounds or anything else.

When you're ready and you want to come out of the hypnotic state, just decide it's time to do so and count up to five slowly in your thoughts, opening your eyes only when you feel completely ready to do so – and if you feel a bit woolly (it's rare but it sometimes happens, and is known as a 'hypnotic hangover') just close your eyes again and repeat the five count more slowly this time before opening your eyes again, when you will feel alert and refreshed.

Change

For most people, when they open their eyes after the session, there's a vague awareness for just a few brief moments that they've been 'someplace else'. It evaporates extremely quickly but it's the best indicator that change has taken place, even if you're not yet fully aware of actually feeling any different.

Change is like that. Sometimes it's immediate, at other times it happens very gradually, almost imperceptibly, so that you are scarcely aware of it at all until you realise that you have somehow managed to achieve that which you were seeking.

It's a magical moment!

Chapter Eighteen

Grief, Loss and Anger

In this final chapter, we have a look first at the nature of grief and the pattern it will usually follow, then at what you can do to help yourself to get through it safely if you ever need to.

This chapter is concerned solely with grief over the physical death of a partner, which is an inevitable part of any relationship that stands the test of time. Some people, particularly those of a spiritual or religious nature, are philosophical about it, especially if there was foreknowledge of the demise as in the case of serious illness. Others, no matter what their belief, are flung into a state of collapse from which they never seem to quite recover.

Between the two extremes is the normal, or usual, process of grief and recovery within which the majority of bereaved individuals experience an oscillation of feelings that vary between denial and anger, depression and eventual acceptance. The entire pattern lasts for around two years and is comprised of four specific stages: *Denial, Anger, Depression, Acceptance.*

Unfortunately, it doesn't run in a chronological fashion and most individuals experience repeated bouts of each of the first three elements in no particular order. This is all completely normal. *Anger* gets directed at nurses, doctors, relatives, self and even the deceased individual themselves. *Denial* has somebody thinking they saw the deceased person walking in the High Street. *Depression* will strike when the sense of hopelessness and loss just becomes too much to tolerate and the mind goes into 'shut down' mode for a while... to be dispelled by another bout of denial or anger. And so it goes on until there is a sudden *Acceptance* of the loss that sometimes happens literally overnight.

It's rare, after that, to return to any of the other three stages, though there can occasionally be 'shadows' of depression for a short while.

For the first three to six months, friends and family will usually be supportive, though will fairly soon begin to subscribe to the belief that: *"They're okay now, they're managing well."* Their visits then become less frequent, their care less evident, and loneliness begins to wreak its havoc; this is where bereavement counselling can provide effective help though no attempt should be made to speed the process up in any way. It is when the symptoms, particularly depression, continue past three years or so that the situation has become one of the two atypical forms – in other words, not following the typical pattern. This is when a therapist with skills and experience in working with unresolved grief can provide inestimable help, and almost any form or psychotherapy, counselling or hypnotherapy can be employed to this end.

Four tasks

The four tasks of mourning, which must be completed in order for the individual to begin to participate fully in life once more, are:

1 To accept the reality of the loss.
2 To work through the pain.
3 To adjust to a life without the deceased.
4 To emotionally relocate the deceased.

The fourth one tends to be where the most difficulties are experienced; guilt and feelings of disloyalty will often work like a complete block to the idea of buying new clothes or furniture, going on holiday, learning new skills, enjoying social occasions or forming new relationships. There might well have been a completion of stage three, adjusting to a life without the deceased, but it is a life *as if* the deceased needs still to be considered. It is almost as if there is a belief that they will be coming back one day. They have not been 'emotionally relocated', that is, the memory and essence of them is still in the everyday brain instead of the part of thoughts where long-departed friends and acquaintances now are... in the memory, just as they should be.

Loyalty to the living is a good thing; loyalty to somebody who is not alive to receive the benefits of it simply creates misery – not a particularly fine testament to a loving relationship. A grieving individual might resist moving on with their life because they are sure the person they've lost wouldn't like it... but even if that were the case, they are no longer around to either approve or disapprove. For an individual to restrict their own enjoyment because of what they believe a deceased partner might have thought is probably a form of self-punishment.

If this is you...

If you are suffering grief right now and less than two years or so have passed since your loss, then it's good to patiently wait it out and prepare for the return to life later on. From time to time, let yourself imagine or think about going out on your own and feeling as if you are a complete individual. There's no need to make any attempt to do that yet. If you feel like talking to the one you have lost, then do so but be at ease if you feel no response... And if you *do* feel some response, allow yourself to wonder if it was real, or if it was created by your subconscious, as a form of comfort that you know your partner would have given if they were able.

The thing is, it doesn't really matter if there's an 'afterwards' or not; currently, you are on this side of any divide and your partner is on the other. Understand and accept that you have a little waiting time before you can let the emotional wound heal completely... and you'll definitely recognise that state when you find it. How you will feel then depends a great deal on your belief system, and it's nobody's business but yours. If you are by nature spiritual or religious, you might view it as having fulfilled your final act of love, or it might seem as if it's permission from your loved one to live again and maybe even love again. Whatever you feel is what you are designed to feel and you can let that feeling be complete and total.

On the other hand, you might be a practical and no-nonsense individual with no particular spiritual or religious belief; in that case, it might just feel as if you have come through a bad time, finally arrived on the other side of it, and you're now ready to pick up the threads of your life again. And that's exactly right for you, no matter what anybody else might say or think.

*You are every bit as valuable a person now as you were before the loss; you might feel different in some way and you might behave differently but you are **you** and you should begin to enjoy every moment of it!*

Atypical grief (1)

There are actually two forms of atypical grief, both with their own difficulties. The first one we will look at is almost exclusively the domain of the **Nomad** individual who might well be the one who gets on with all the funeral arrangements and musters the family together. They seem not to feel the same depth of despair as others (though they might be simply disguising it) and are able to keep their act together when all around them are losing it. Sometimes, they collapse quietly in private, so that nobody knows, since they are often averse to showing despair. At other times, they move on to the next stage of life and might amaze or offend others by the undue haste with which they embark on a new relationship – and that is probably an inherited trait from the Nomads of old who, under duress, would journey to somewhere new. There are actually three types of Nomad grief:

- Apparently lighthearted in mood, but with hidden pain.
- Evidently displayed, showing more emotion than others might.
- Transient and philosophical moving on quite quickly.

If any one of those is you, just accept that it is the authentic you – you didn't choose it and cannot choose to change it, though for the sake of the sensibilities of others you might decide to normalise it a little, at least on the surface.

If, instead, you see one of these patterns from the outside, remember that the person concerned cannot genuinely change what they feel any more than you can. If they seem to you to be disrespectful or flippant, it's merely your interpretation of their behaviour as what it would mean if it was you behaving like that. But they aren't you and the depth of feeling anybody experiences is only what they *can* experience under any given set of circumstances. We can't choose to feel more, or less, about anything and we should resist any temptation to attempt to make others do so. If you appear to be feeling more than they seem to be, and it seems to you that you have it right, then be pleased that you have a more complete set of emotions.

Atypical grief (2)

In this situation, the grieving individual fails to work through the processes of grief and might even seem to be resisting moving on. It's not a matter of choice and it's not at all unusual for the individual concerned to be unaware that they are stuck somewhere in the grief process. If you are wondering if this is you, there are some indicators – though none of these is really relevant until three years or more have passed:

- You have their telephone number still stored in your mobile.
- You sometimes talk to them as if they are just in another

room.
- You occasionally tell yourself they are simply working away from home.
- Their clothes are still hanging in the wardrobe.
- You wonder if they will approve of something.
- You sometimes feel them 'around'.
- You don't feel as if you are really 'part of the world'.

There are many others but these are the main ones. The more of these you can identify with, the more likely it is that you are suffering unresolved grief, and you are most likely a **Warrior** personality. The warrior tends sometimes to 'take pleasure in unpleasure' and will therefore be unwilling to let go of the pain. Also, you might still be harbouring some anger at somebody associated with the death, even your partner themselves. But that anger is only hurting you, not punishing anybody else – in fact, the object of your anger is unlikely to even know that you feel it... so you can afford to let it go to wherever anger goes when it's finally released.

Releasing your unresolved grief is beyond the scope of this book, but you can find some help from a psychotherapist, counsellor or hypnotherapist with relevant training, or you can approach one of the specialist organisations listed in the **'Resources'** pages at the end of the book.

Mortality fear

This last section has little to do directly with love or sex but is included here to help those who have lost somebody and suffering fears about their own demise.

Sometimes, experiencing bereavement and subsequent grief creates a huge shock to the subconscious that can trigger crippling fears of our own mortality. To fear death is part of the 'human condition' and an inherited instinct, since those of our ancestors who didn't have it would not have survived very long at all. If you find yourself in this situation, it is worth consulting with somebody with experience of working with 'existential anxiety' – essentially, a fear of death.

In the meantime, bear in mind that none of us have any knowledge at all about what happens when we die. Some people think they have but there's no evidence. Maybe there's nothing for us after death in the same way as there was nothing for us before we were born; maybe there's one of the various forms of Heaven, which those who have had Near Death Experiences would have us believe – it certainly proves impossible to shake their belief that they have seen 'the other side'. Or perhaps we live many lives, as in the Buddhist belief system until we have achieved Nirvana.

There is much anecdotal evidence of consciousness surviving after physical death but it is still only anecdotal and the only thing that's certain is that we will all find out eventually. Or maybe not.

The Beginning

A whole brand new start

'The Beginning' might seem a rather curious title for this last – rather short – section of the book but it actually describes perfectly where you might find yourself right now... at the beginning of a better life than you had before you started reading.

You've learnt much about yourself and about how that self came to be, and hopefully have stopped any self-recrimination about the way you feel and what you truly want from life. You've discovered that you're most certainly not weird or awkward and that you deserve, just like everybody else, to find sex, love and happiness in a relationship, and how to do your bit to keep everything running as smoothly as a well-maintained machine. Because that's what a relationship is – a machine with only two moving parts where there is enough leeway for one of those parts to occasionally malfunction without the whole thing becoming a total write-off.

This book is effectively a toolkit that will help you to make repairs when necessary and adjustments and enhancements where possible, yet confidently find and drive a brand new model when that's the best choice for you to make. Never again will you need to suffer the discomfort of prolonging a situation in the vain hope of a miracle cure for what ails it, and nor will you need to enter into a relationship without any idea of how well life might work with the individual you have your eye on. And you even have the resources to let you chat up a stranger without awkwardness!

In short, you have the beginning of an understanding of how to handle relationships of all sorts, with their embarrassments, their arguments, their wild passions and their deepest sorrows... and come up smiling.

Good Luck!

Resources

There is no claim that the organisations listed here are preferred or in some way better than others, only that they are known to be reputable.

Relate: http://www.relate.org.uk
Counselling (BACP): http://www.bacp.co.uk/
Psychotherapy (UKCP): http://www.psychotherapy.org.uk
Hypnotherapy: http://www.hypnotherapy-directory.org.uk
The Complementary and Natural Healthcare Council: http://www.cnhc.org.uk
Meridian therapy: http://theamt.com
Neuro-Linguistic Programming (NLP): http://www.anlp.org
Cognitive Behavioural Therapy (CBT): http://www.mind.org.uk/mental_health_a-z/8000_cognitive_behaviour_therapy
For help with leaving an abusive partner: http://refuge.org.uk
Legal advice: http://www.citizensadvice.org.uk

Some private organisations that might be helpful:
The following are known to be reputable associations of therapists in the UK who have a strict code of ethics to which their members must adhere:

The Association for Professional Hypnosis and Psychotherapy: http://www.aphp.co.uk

The National Council for Hypnotherapy: http://www.hypnotherapists.org.uk

The (British) National Register of Advanced Hypnotherapists http://www.nrah.co.uk

WSN Counselling & Coaching – *an exclusive register of therapists trained to the highest level in the 'Warriors, Settlers & Nomads'*

therapy. http://www.wsn-counselling.co.uk/

The National register of Psychotherapists and Counsellors: http://www.nrpc.co.uk

For information on Near Death Experiences: http://www .nderf.org

Bibliography

Warriors, Settlers & Nomads (2000) Terence Watts, Crown House, Swansea, UK

Rapid Cognitive Therapy (1999) Terence Watts and Georges Phillips, Crown House,
Swansea, UK

Memories, Dream and Reflections (1962) C.J. Jung, Collins, London, UK

Psychological Testing (1988) Anne Anastasi, Collier Macmillan, London

The Psychopathology of Everyday Life (orig. 1901, first British ed. 1914) Freud, Penguin Books, London

Charles Darwin's Notebooks, Paul Barrett (ed.) 1987, Cambridge University Press

Other books by Terence Watts

Rapid Cognitive Therapy
Warriors, Settlers & Nomads
HYPNOSIS: Advanced Techniaques in Hypnosis and
Hypnoanalysis
Magic! for Minds
7 Ways and 7 Days to Banish Your Anxiety
Various professional text books

PSYCHE BOOKS

The study of the mind: interactions, behaviours, functions. Developing and learning our understanding of self. Psyche Books cover all aspects of psychology and matters relating to the head.